FOREIGN
LANGUAGE COURSES

Power-Glide
Children's German Level III

Activity Book

by

Robert W. Blair

This product would not have been possible without the assistance of many people. The help of those mentioned below was invaluable.

Editorial, Design and Production Staff

Instructional Design: Robert Blair, Ph.D.

Project Coordinator: James Blair

Development Manager: David Higginbotham

Story Writer: Natalie Prado

Cover Design: Guy Francis

Contributing Editors: Gretchen Hilton, Emily Spackman, Ann Dee Knight, Heather Monson, Amelia Taylor

Audios Voices: Jorg Bachmann, Jenny Dean, Fabian Fulda, Cindy Renker, Ross Storey

Illustrator: Apryl Robertson

Translators: Christel Marie Secrist

Musicians: Geoff Groberg, Rob Bird

Audio Recording, Editing and Mixing: Rob Bird

Power-Glide Foreign Language Courses
1682 W 820 N, Provo, UT 84601
(4/02)

Contents

Introduction 4
The Adventure Continues 8
Diglot Weave Review 10
Meister Gänsedieb 12
Reizender Schmetterling 15
The Three Bears I . . . .
   Scatter Chart 18
   Diglot Weave 21
   Review Questions 27
The Three Bears II . . . .
   Diglot Weave 28
   Story Telling 32
Word Puzzle 1 35
The Dog, the Cat and the Mouse I . . . .
   Diglot Weave 37
   Scatter Chart 39
The Dog, the Cat and the Mouse II . . . .
   Diglot Weave 41
   Story Telling 44
Word Puzzle 2 46
Hard Days . . . .
   Horseshoe Story 49
   Scatter Chart 51
Mystery Map 53
Manuscripts! 56
Test 1 58
Answer Key 62
The Adventure Continues 64
Wenn der Pott aber nun ein Loch hat .65
Bei Goldhähnchen 70
The Hunter and the Thief I . . . .
   Match and Learn 73
   Diglot Weave 75
   Review Questions 77
The Hunter and the Thief II . . . .
   Diglot Weave 78
   Story Telling 80
Word Puzzle 3 82
A Boy and His Goat I . . . .
   Scatter Chart 84
   Diglot Weave 86
   Review Questions 90
A Boy and His Goat II . . . .
   Diglot Weave 91
Word Puzzle 4 96
A Sandwich in the Universe . . . .
   Horseshoe story 98
   Scatter Chart 100
   Story telling 103
Final Word Puzzle 104
Success! 107
Safe Return 109
Test 2 110
Answer Key 114
Recipes 115

A Note to Parents

Basic Course Objectives

The major goal of this course is to keep children excited about communicating in another language. The adventure story, the variety of activities, and the simplified teaching methods employed in the course are all designed to make learning interesting and fun.

This course is primarily for children 2nd through 4th grade. Course activities are designed specifically with these learners in mind and include matching games, story telling, speaking, drawing, creative and deductive thinking, acting, and guessing—all things which children do for fun!

Ultimately, children who complete the course can expect to understand an impressive amount of German, including common German phrases, complete German sentences, German numbers, rhymes, and questions. They will also be able to understand stories told all or mostly in German, to retell these stories themselves using German, and to make up stories of their own using words and sentence patterns they have learned.

Children who complete the course will be well prepared to continue learning with our other German courses, and they will have the foundation that will make learning at that level just as fun and interesting, albeit more challenging, as in this course.

Teaching Techniques

This course allows your children to learn by doing, to learn through enjoyable experiences. The idea is to put the experience first and the explanation after. This is important to note because it is directly opposite to how teaching—and especially foreign language teaching—is traditionally done. Typically foreign language teachers spend the majority of their time explaining complex grammar and syntax rules, and drilling students on vocabulary. In this traditional mode, rules and lists come first and experience comes last. Learning experientially, on the other hand, simulates the natural language acquisition process of children.

When children learn their native languages apparently effortlessly in early childhood, it is not through the study of grammar rules and vocabulary lists. Rather, they learn the words for things around them simply by listening to others, and they intuitively grasp an amazing amount of grammar and syntax in the same way. By using activities that simulate natural language acquisition, it is not only possible but normal for children to learn a new language quickly and enjoy doing it!

Specifically, this course motivates your children to learn German by providing learning experiences in the form of matching games, story telling exercises, drawing exercises, singing and acting, and other fun activities aimed at developing functional language comprehension and speaking ability. These activities contrast markedly with the exercises in more traditional courses, which tend to focus exclusively on learning some vocabulary, or on understanding very simple German sentences, without extending learning to the point of actually understanding and speaking the language. The language your children will acquire through this course will be more useful to them than language learned through traditional approaches, because knowledge gained in fun, rather than stressful, ways is much easier for children to retain and much more natural for them to use themselves.

Using the Course

This course is carefully designed so that it can be used either by children working primarily on their own or by parents and children working closely together. Complete instructions, simple enough to be easily followed by children, are included on the audios. Parents or other adults can enhance the course significantly by acting as facilitators: reviewing instructions, encouraging creativity and course participation, providing frequent opportunities for children to display what they have learned, rewarding effort and accomplishment, and providing enthusiasm. Keep in mind that much of the real learning takes place as you interact with your children during and after the course learning experiences.

Perhaps the most important of the above ways parents can help their children is to give them an audience for their new skills. In order to facilitate this invaluable help, we have added a new feature to the Children's Level III German Course. At the end of each activity or story we have included suggestions for a Performance Challenge. One goal of Power-Glide courses is to teach students to produce the target language creatively and independently. The new Performance Challenge feature will help children do just that. These additional exercises will increase your child's fluency, pronunciation, and confidence in the target language, as well as give you the opportunity to be directly involved in the learning process. Encourage your children to use as much German as possible and give them the audience they need to perform for. Remind your students not to worry about mistakes. Rather, encourage them to review any words they may struggle with and make sure they feel comfortable with the current material before moving to the next lesson.

Using the resources provided in the course book and on the audios, an adult learning facilitator does not need to know German or how to teach it in order to be a great learning partner. In fact, one of the most enjoyable and effective ways to learn is together, as a team.

Parents or other adults who know German can, of course, supplement the materials in this course very effectively. A proficient bilingual teacher could, for example: (1) help children learn additional vocabulary by putting several objects on table and asking and answering questions about them, such as "What is this?" or "Where is the _____?", and so on; (2) create on-the-spot diglot-weave stories by reading illustrated children's books such as Silverstein's *Are You My Mother?*, putting key words (picturable nouns) into German, and asking questions about the story or its pictures partly or completely in German; (3) involve children in making and doing things (such as making a paper airplane or finding a hidden object) giving instructions all or partly in German.

We have added another new feature to this course that will make it easier to use. For each audio track, you will see a CD icon that includes the CD number and the track number. This will help you to easily find your place from lesson to lesson.

Benefits of Second Language Acquisition

Learning a second language has many benefits. Besides the obvious value of being able to understand and communicate with others, research in the United States and Canada in the 1970s and '80s has shown that learning a second language gives children a distinct advantage in general school subject areas. Seeing linguistic and cultural contrasts as they acquire a second language, children gain insight not only into the new language and cultures, but into their own language and culture as well.

Furthermore, a considerable amount of research has shown that learning a second language in childhood helps children learn to read and write their native language. Quite possibly the best phonics training a child can receive is to learn a language like German, because German spelling is quite phonetic: when one knows German, the spelling of a German word tells him or her how to pronounce it, and (with few exceptions) the sound of a German word tells him or her how to spell it. This carries over to English and helps children intuitively understand how language works.

Our Goal

Our goal at Power-Glide is to change the way the U.S. studies language. We want to produce foreign language speakers, not just studiers. This Children's Level III German Course effectively continues the road to speaking German. We hope you and your children will find delight in the ongoing adventure of learning another language.

The Adventure Continues

(*Vienna*)

Track 1

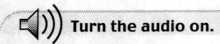 **Turn the audio on.**

Narrator: You and your Onkel Otto and cousin Margarethe enter the Danube National Park in Vienna, Austria. You are so excited. Ever since you landed in Vienna last night, you have been eager to explore the city. The first place you head is the National Park, where your Onkel thinks Heinrich Trapp, the notorious trickster who stole the ancient Bach scores, might have hidden the next clue in the puzzle. The park is pristine and beautiful, green and lush.

Otto: Okay, Tony, Lisa, here's what we need to do. The manuscript that Herr Trapp left in his journals indicates that the next clue will be hidden "im Zahn des Tigers."

Tony: Let's see… "Tiger" means "tiger", I remember that.

Margarethe: That's right. "Im Zahn des Tigers" means "in the tiger's tooth."

Lisa: Okay, so we need to find something that looks like a tiger. Let's go.

Narrator: You begin looking, but you start to get discouraged after a couple of hours, and you are more distracted by the park than you are by the clue. You both run around all the winding paths and peer into the murky riverbed. At one point you even see a mud turtle slipping into the water. Your Onkel Otto tells you these turtles are very rare, on the verge of extinction. By noon, you are very tired and are almost ready to give up your search.

Lisa: I don't know if we're going to find anything.

Tony: Me neither. We should… hey! Look over there! Doesn't that rock kind of look like a tiger's head?

Lisa: You're right! Let's go take a look.

Narrator: You both climb up a slippery incline to where a large rock, which really does look like a tiger throwing back its head to roar, is cropping out of the hillside. Up close, the head is actually pretty scary, and you hesitate.

Tony: Do you really think we need to put our hands inside the mouth? It's kind of creepy.

Lisa: Well, the clue is in the Zahn, and I don't think we'll find any teeth outside the mouth. Come on.

Narrator: You nervously stick your hand into the dark open mouth of rock and feel around.

Lisa: What's that?

Narrator: You pull out a piece of parchment, with writing on it in German.

Tony: We did it! We found the clue! Let's go show Onkel Otto und Margarethe.

Narrator: You run over to your Onkel, who is impressed with how quickly you found the clue.

Margarethe: What does the clue say, Vater?

Otto: It says, "Schau unter den Bären, die dort wachsen, wohin die Gänsediebe es nicht wagen zu gehen und wo Schmetterlinge frei fliegen."

Tony: What does that mean?

Otto: I'm not sure. Let's head back zu dem Hotel.

 Turn the audio off.

Three Pigs, Chicken Little, Circus Act Mantis & the Butterfly

(Diglot Weave Review)

Track 2

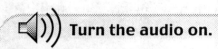 **Turn the audio on.**

Narrator: Onkel Otto drives back to the hotel through the cobblestone streets of Vienna. You sit in back, with your nose stuck to the window. Everything in this part of the city looks old, as though it hasn't changed in a hundred years. You stare eagerly at all of the statues and cathedrals you pass.

Tony: This is so much fun! I can't wait to explore the city.

Lisa: Can we go see some sights later on today?

Otto: Maybe, if we have time, but remember why I agreed to bring you on this trip to Austria, Österreich. You must learn as much German as you can, and we must find those Bach papers. Right?

Tony: Yes, of course, Onkel Otto, but we have been learning a lot.

Otto: Really? Do you remember everything you've learned?

Lisa: I think so.

Otto: Okay. Let's see if you remember one of the first stories in German I ever taught you. Do you remember Das zerbrochene Fenster?

Lisa: Um…

Tony: Let's see…

Margarethe: That was a long time ago, Vater.

Otto: Yes, that's true. Let's review some of the stories we've learned so far so that you're ready to solve this puzzle with me. Ready?

Track 3

Es waren einmal drei kleine Schweine. Die drei kleine Schweine are brothers, Brüder. They each built ein Haus—ein Haus aus Stroh, ein Haus aus Zweigen, und ein Haus aus Ziegelsteinen. Eines Tages, ein Wolf came. He went to dem Haus aus Stroh, dem Haus von Bruder Nummer drei und told dem Kleinen Schwein to let him rein or he'd blasen und blasen and destroy his house. Der dritte Bruder wouldn't let den Wolf ein, so the wolf huffed and puffed and destroyed his Haus aus Stroh. Der dritte

Bruder entkam, though, and ran to dem haus von dem zweiten Bruder, dem Haus aus Zweigen. Aber der Wolf came to this Haus, too, and made the same demand. Der zweite Bruder wouldn't let den Wolf in sein Haus, either, so der Wolf huffed and puffed and destroyed das Haus aus Zweigen. Fortunately, die zwei kleinen Schweine escaped and ran to dem Haus von dem ersten Bruder, dem Haus aus Ziegesteinen. Der Wolf followed them but couldn't catch them, so er came to dem Haus aus Ziegesteinen and knocked on die Tür and made the same demands, but der erste Bruder wouldn't listen to dem Wolf, either, so der Wolf huffed and puffed and puffed and huffed, aber he couldn't destroy das Haus aus Ziegesteinen. Der Wolf had to go home sehr, sehr hungrig.

And on the way home, der Wolf sees something very strange. He sees einen Elefaunten auf der Erdestehen. Then ein Tiger springt auf dem Rücken von dem Elefaunten. Ein Hund springt auf den Rücken des Tigers. Ein Affe springt auf den Rücken des Hundes. Eine Katze springt auf den Rücken des Affens. Suddenly, ein Maus rennt über dem Boden. Then all die Tiere jump down und jagen die Maus. Aber die Maus entkommt. Die Maus hat großes Glück!

As it runs toward its comfortable hole in an old barn, die Maus sees a group of animals. It sees ein Küken, eine Henne, eine Ente, eine Gans, ein Trughahn, und ein Fuchs. All die Teire except dem Fuchs are saying that der Himmel fällt. Die Tiere follow dem Fuchs into seine Höhle, and none of them come back out. So die Maus keeps running. It doesn't want der Fuchs to eat it, too.

Die Maus stops to rest under a tree, and when it looks up, it sees another strange scene unfolding in the tree. Aüf dem Baum gibes ein Blatt. Auf dem Blatt gibt es ein Schmetterling. Hinter dem Schmetterling gibt es eine Gottesanbeterin. Hinter der Gottesanbeterin ist ein Vogel. Hinter dem Vogel gibt es eine Katze. Hinter dem Katze gibt es eine Schlange. Die Schlange will die Katze fressen. Die Katze will den Vogel fressen. Der Vogel will die Gottesanbeterin fressen. Die Gottesanbeterin will den Schmetterling fressen. Was wird geschehen? Der Schmetterling siegt die Gottesanbeterin und fliegt weg. Die Gottesanbeterin verliert ihr Essen. Der Vogel fliegt zu einem anderen Zweig. Die Katze springt aus dem Baum. Die Schlange rollt sich auseinder und schleicht weg. Die Maus ist glücklich that the pretty Schmetterling entkommt.

 Turn the audio off.

Meister Gänsedieb

(Ditties)

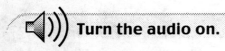 **Turn the audio on.**

Narrator: When you arrive at your hotel, you all race up to your room, to try and see if you can find out what the next clue means. When you get to your door, however, you hesitate.

Margarethe: What is it? Is something wrong?

Otto: Look, Margarethe, die Tür is open. I'm sure I locked it when we left.

Narrator: You are suddenly very nervous as you creep over to the door and look past it. Inside the hotel room, all of your belongings are scattered across the floor, with papers everywhere and chairs knocked over.

Margarethe: We've been robbed! This is terrible.

Otto: Yes… look! They've taken Herr Trapp's manuscript with all the clues to the mystery in it!

Margarethe: Look, all our money is here, though. It must have been the manuscripts they were after. Why?

Otto: It must be someone who is also searching for the Bach musical scores. Do you remember? I told a friend I trusted about the manuscript, and he betrayed me to search for it himself. I believe he's the one who took it.

Tony: That's terrible! Wie heißt er?

Otto: His name is Nikolaus, and we went to school together in Berlin. He's the only person I can think of who knew I had Herr Trapp's clues.

Lisa: What will happen if he finds the Bach papers?

Otto: He will probably sell them to an antique collector, instead of giving them to the Berlin Museum, where they belong. These papers are a national treasure, and they belong to the German people, not just to the rich.

Tony: Is there any way that we can still find the papers before Nikolaus?

Otto: It would be very difficult. He would have the advantage over us, because he has the clues. We would have to work from memory.

Lisa: Still, we have the clue from the tiger's tooth. Do you think that will help us?

Margarethe: Of course! We still have a chance!

Otto: That's true, and we have all of my folklore research to help us as well. In fact, I think I know a song that might help us with the clue. Let me see... here it is, luckily he didn't take any of my research. Are you ready to learn the song so that we can solve the clue?

Lisa & Tony: Ja!

Otto: Okay. This is how the first part goes:
Wer eine Gans gestohlen hat,
Der ist ein Dieb,
Und wer sie mir dann wiederbringt,
Den hab' ich lieb.
Da steht der Gänsedieb,
Den hat kein Mensch mehr lieb.
Sing that with me.

All:
Wer eine Gans gestohlen hat,
Der ist ein Dieb,
Und wer sie mir dann wiederbringt,
Den hab' ich lieb.
Da steht der Gänsedieb,
Den hat kein Mensch mehr lieb.

Otto: Great. Let's see, how does the second part go?

Margarethe: I remember, Vater. Listen.
Wir wünschen Glück
Zu Deinem neuen Orden,
Daß du bist
Ein Gänsedieb geworden.
Viel Glück, Meister Gänsedieb,
Viel Glück, Meister Gänsedieb,
Viel Glück!

Otto: That's right. Let's sing it together.

All:
Wir wünschen Glück
Zu Deinem neuen Orden,
Daß du bist
Ein Gänsedieb geworden.
Viel Glück, Meister Gänsedieb,
Viel Glück, Meister Gänsedieb,

Viel Glück!

Margarethe: Good! Let's sing through the whole thing now.

All:
Wer eine Gans gestohlen hat,
Der ist ein Dieb,
Und wer sie mir dann wiederbringt,
Den hab' ich lieb.
Da steht der Gänsedieb,
Den hat kein Mensch mehr lieb.
Wir wünschen Glück
Zu Deinem neuen Orden,
Daß du bist
Ein Gänsedieb geworden.
Viel Glück, Meister Gänsedieb,
Viel Glück, Meister Gänsedieb,
Viel Glück!

Margarethe: Sehr gut!

 Turn the audio off.

Performance Challenge:

Now that you have learned a new song, share your German with a parent, friend, or one of your brothers and sisters by teaching them the song. Remember to teach it in German and then translate the words into English if your partner does not understand German. For an even greater challenge, try writing a song about your culture and put it to the tune of the German song you just learned. If you need an idea to get you started, just think of what a visitor from another country would like to know about you and your family.

Reizender Schmetterling...
(Ditties)

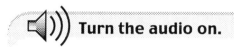 **Turn the audio on.**

Track 5

Tony: Okay, Onkel Otto, we understand about "den Gänsedieb" but what about "wo Schmetterlinge frei Fliegen"? And what about the growing "Bären"?

Margarethe: Let me think… There's that story about some Bären, but I don't know if Tony and Lisa are quite ready for it yet. I think I remember one song you found a couple of years ago, Vater, that had to do with "Schmetterlinge." What was it? Something about "Reizender Schmetterling…"

Otto: Hmm, let me see… I'm sorry, Margarethe, but I don't think I know that one.

Margarethe: It started off, "Reizender Schmetterling, Flüchtiges, kleines Ding…"

Otto: Oh, that one! Let's see, I remember some of the words, but I just don't remember the whole thing.

Tony: Well, tell us the part you do remember. Maybe that will be enough for us to get the clue.

Otto: Very well. I think this is the first verse. Listen closely.
Reizender Schmetterling,
Flüchtiges, kleines Ding,
Willst du nicht einmal ruhn,
Mir es zu Liebe tun,
Daß ich gemütlich kann
Schauen dein Kleidchen an?
Reizender Schmetterling,
Flüchtiges, kleines Ding,
Schmetterling, setz' dich!

Lisa: That's easy! Let me try.

Otto: All right. It's harder without the melody. Do your best Lisa!

Lisa:
Reizender Schmetterling,
Flüchtiges, kleines Ding,
Willst du nicht einmal ruhn,
Mir es zu Liebe tun,
Daß ich gemütlich kann
Schauen dein Kleidchen an?

Reizender Schmetterling,
Flüchtiges, kleines Ding,
Schmetterling, setz' dich!

Otto: Gut. Sehr gut. I'm sorry I don't remember the rest, children.

Lisa: That's okay. Let's take another look at the clue and see if we understand it now.

 Turn the audio off.

Performance Challenge:

Now that you have learned a new song, share your German with a parent, friend, or one of your brothers and sisters by teaching them the song. Remember to teach it in German and then translate the words into English if your partner does not understand German. For an even greater challenge, try writing a song about your culture and put it to the tune of the German song you just learned. If you need an idea to get you started, just think of what a visitor from another country would like to know about you and your family.

The Three Bears I

(Scatter Chart)

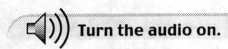 **Turn the audio on.**

Narrator: You sit down to try and figure out the clue.

Tony: Let's see, what was the clue again?

Margarethe: "Schau unter den Bären, die dort wachsen, wohin die Gänsediebe es nicht wagen zu gehen und wo Schmetterlinge frei fliegen."

Lisa: But where would a goose thief not want to go? There are lots of places with no geese.

Tony: It doesn't say that goose thieves wouldn't want to go to this place, it says they wouldn't dare go to it. That means we probably want a place with lots of geese that somehow makes goose thieves want to stay away.

Lisa: An old prison, maybe? Are there any old prisons that keep geese?

Otto: Not that I know of.

Lisa: A courthouse, then, or maybe a castle?

Margarethe: Now, there's an idea. Vater, do you think the clue could be talking about the Schönbrunn?

Otto: Possibly. Herr Trapp stayed in the Schönbrunn's west wing for several years, before the emperor found out what a rogue he was.

Tony: Do they have geese there?

Otto: Yes. There are many geese in the Schloss gardens.

Lisa: But no goose thief would dare to take them from right under the emperor's nose.

Tony: Right! But what about the butterflies?

Lisa: Well, any place with lots of gardens probably has lots of butterflies.

Tony: Flying freely?

Lisa: Why not?

Tony: What about the growing bears? I doubt the Schloss has any live bears in the gardens.

Lisa: We'll worry about that when we get there. Besides, Onkel Otto still needs to teach us the story about the bears. We'll know what to look for after he's taught us.

Otto: Well, children, Margarethe, I do believe you're right. Shall we pay a visit to the Schönbrunn?

Tony & Lisa: Ja!

Narrator: As you begin to drive to the Schloss, it is just striking noon. You are driving by the Hoher Markt, and there is a huge clock outside. As the bells toll, life-sized figures come out of the clock, like a huge wind-up toy, and dance around.

Tony: What is that, Onkel Otto?

Otto: That is the "Anker Clock." It's amazing isn't it?

Margarethe: Just wait until you see Schönbrunn.

Narrator: You can't wait to see what other delights Vienna—Wien—has to offer, and are peering out the window when the Schloss comes into view. It is enormous, and the reflecting pool lying in front of it makes it seem even more so.

Otto: Schönbrunn was the Schloss of Emperor Franz Joseph. He was born here in 1830.

Lisa: But, it's huge! How will we know what to look for?

Otto: Well, from what I remember in the manuscript, there is an old folk tale that Herr Trapp associated with his stay at this Schloss. Would you like to hear it?

Tony: Yeah. We'll need to know it if we're going to find the next clue.

Otto: Okay, listen. Here are some words you're going to need to know in order to understand the story.

Look at the pictures on your workbook page and point to what you hear.

Track 7

die drei Bären
the three bears

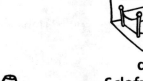
das Sclafzimmer
the bedroom

brüllte
roared

das Wohnzimmer
the living room

die Schüsseln
the bowls

die Küche
the kitchen

das Bett
the bed

das Baby-Bärchen
the baby bear

die Tür
the door

der Vati Bär
the father bear

die Mutti Bären
the mother bear

der Stuhle
the chair

jemand
someone

der Tisch
the table

der Löffel
the spoon

der Brei
the mush

🔊 **Turn the audio off.**

Performance Challenge:

Choose five of the new words and pictures that you learned in the Scatter Chart. Show the pictures to a parent, friend, or one of your brothers and sisters and explain to them how you think the picture represents the words you have learned. For an even greater challenge, create your own story using the pictures. Bring out the artist in yourself by drawing your own versions of the pictographs and making a book with the story you create.

The Three Bears I
(Diglot Weave)

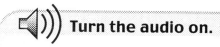 **Turn the audio on.**

Track 8

Narrator: After you park, you begin the walk up to Schönbrunn. As you enter, you marvel at the gorgeous decorations and panels that line the walls.

Lisa: How can we be sure that this is where the next clue will be? Do you think we understood wrong?

Otto: Maybe, but I hope that we're right. If Nikolaus is going to the right place and we're not, then he will definitely find the clue before we do. However, if this is the right place, I think I know what part of the palace—Schloss—the next clue would be. When Nikolaus stayed here, he stayed in the west part of the Schloss. That's where I think we should look. How I wish we still had the memoirs!

Narrator: You agree with your Onkel, but you all begin to head to the west wing together.

Otto: Kinder! Schnell!

Narrator: Your Onkel pulls you all into a doorway, out of the corridor.

Tony: Was gibt's, Onkel Otto?

Otto: I thought I saw… yes, look there.

Narrator: You cautiously peek out into the hallway, where you see a middle-aged man with graying blonde hair walk past without seeing you.

Margarethe: It's Nikolaus!

Lisa: Oh, no! Does that mean he has the clue?

Otto: I doubt it. If he had found it, he would be heading toward the exit, not away from it. In any case, at least we know we're in the right place.

Tony: Shouldn't we learn the story, so that we know what to look for?

Otto: You're right, Tony. Let's go over the first version.

Track 9

Die Geschichte von Goldlöchen und die drei Bären

This is the berühmte 📖 about 🧸 und Goldlöchen. As in other children's

stories, diese 📖 begins with the words: es war einmal...once upon a time. Now hör

die 📖.

Es waren einmal 🧸. They lived in einem 🏠 in the forest...im 🌲. If

you know die 📖 Geschichte von den 🐻, you know what ein 🏠 is. Ein

🌲 is where die 🐺 and die 🐻 and other 🐕 live, isn't it? 🧸 are

🐻 , 🐻 , und 🐻 .

One morning, 🐻 cooked up a nice pot of oatmeal 🥣 . Then she set 🪑

with drie 🥣 und drei 🥄 : eine große 🥣 und ein großer 🥄 für den

🐻 , und ein mittelgroße 🥣 , und ein mittelgroße 🥄 for herself, und eine

kleine 🥣 und ein kleine 🥄 für das 🐻 . She filled 🥣 with the hot

🥣 und called out, "Vatibär, Babybärchen, kommt und esst...come and eat!"

🐻 sat down at 🪑 , picked up his großen 🥄 , und tasted den 🥣 in

seiner großen 🥣 . "Mensch! Too hot, der 🥣 is too hot," sagte er.

🐻 sat down at 🪑 , picked up her mittelgroßen 🥄 , und tasted 🥣

in ihrer mittelgroßen 🥣 . "Auha! Ja, der 🥣 ist too hot," sagte sie .

🐻 sat down at den 🪑 , picked up seinen kleinen 🥄 , und tasted

🥣 . "Auah! Ja, der 🥣 ist is too hot," sagte er.

Then  sagte, "I say, let's go take a walk im 🌳."

🐻 sagte, "Oh yes, let's take a walk im 🌳."

🐻 sagte, "Oh, yes, let's for a walk im 🌳."

Then 🐻 , 🐻 , und 🐻 went out to take a walk im 🌳.

Aber they forgot to lock 🚪. Oh-oh!

Now, while 🐻🐻 were walking im 🌳, ein kleines Mädchen came by. It was

Goldlöchen. She saw 🏠 der 🐻🐻. Not knowing that it was 🏠 der 🐻🐻, she

knocked on 🚪. No one came.

She opened 🚪 und called out, "You-hou!" No one answered. So she entered

ins 🏠. Oh my! Meine Güte! First, she went into 🪑. There she saw 🥣🥣 auf

dem 🪑.

"I'm hungry," sagte sie. "Ich habe Hunger. I think no one will mind if I taste

this 🥣. Then Goldlöchen sat down at den 🪑, took den großen 🥄, und tasted

🥣 in der großen 🥣 , 🥣 des 🐻. "Auah! Dieser 🥣 ist too hot!"

sagte sie.

Then she went over und took den mittelgroßen 🥄 und tasted den 🥣 in

der mittelgroßen 🥣 , 🥣 der 🐻 . "Auah!" sagte sie. "Dieser 🥣 ist too

hot!"

Then she went over und took den kleinen Löffel 🥄 und tasted den 🥣 in der 🥣 des 🐻 .. "Ah!" sagte sie. "Dieser 🥣 ist just right." And without think-

ing, Goldlöchen ate it all up.

Then she went into the living room... 🛋️ . There she sah drei Stühle: einen

großen 🪑 , den 🪑 des 🐻 ; einene mittelgroßen 🪑 , den 🪑

der 🐻 ; und einen kleinen 🪑 , den 🪑 des 🐻 . First, Goldlöchen sat down

on den großen 🪑 . "Auah! Dieser 🪑 ist too hard," sagte sie.

Then she went over et sat down on den mittelgroßen 🪑 . "Auah!

Dieser 🪑 ist too soft," sagte sie.

Then she went over et sat down on den kleinen 🪑 ,den 🪑 des 🐻 .

"Ah! Dieser 🪑 ist just right," sagte sie. She leaned back und CRACK! der 🪑 broke.

What a pity! Schade!

She picked herself up and went upstairs to dem 🪟 . There she sah drei Betten:

ein großes 🛏️ , 🛏️ des 🐻 ; ein mittelgroßen 🛏️ , 🛏️ der 🐻 ; und

ein kleines 🛏️ , 🛏️ des 🐻 .

First, Goldilocks lay down on das große 🛏️ , 🛏️ der 🐻 ."Auah!" sagte

sie. "Dieses 🛏️ ist too hard."

Then she went over und sat down on das mittelgroße 🛏️ , 🛏️ der 🐻 .

"Oh! Dieses 🛏️ ist too soft," sagte sie.

Then she went over und lay down on das kleine 🛏️ , 🛏️ des 🐻 . "Ah!"

sagte sie. "Dieses ist just right, and I am very tired." Then she laid her head on the pillow und soon fell asleep.

Just then returned from their walk im . First they went into .

There sah seine und sagte, "Oh-oh! Somebody has tasted meinen ."

sah ihre und sagte, "Oh-oh! Somebody has tasted meinen ."

sah seine und sagte, "Oh-oh! Somebody has tasted meinen , too, and has eaten it all up." Und began to cry.

Then went into . looked at seinen großen und , " has sat auf meinem ."

looked at ihren mittelgroßen und sagte, " has sat auf meinem ."

looked at seinen kleinen und sagte, " has sat auf meinem , too, and broke it. Look!" Und das began to cry.

Then went upstairs. looked atsein großes und , " has lain in meinem ."

looked at ihr mittelgroßes und sagte, " has lain in meinem , also."

looked at sein kleines und sagte, " has lain in meinem , also...and HERE SHE IS!"

At that moment, Goldlöchen woke up and schrie, "AAAAAH!"

Then she jumped out of dem *und lief nach Hause as fast as she could.*

 didn't chase after her. *went down to* *und reheated* *.*

went down to *und fixed dem Kaputten* *.* *stopped crying.*

And as for Goldlöchen, she never walked alone im 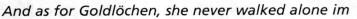 *after*

that.

🔊 **Turn the audio off.**

Performance Challenge:

There are four parts to this Performance Challenge:
1. Read the story silently to yourself.
2. Read the story aloud to yourself.
3. Read the story aloud to a parent, friend or one of your brothers and sisters.
4. Retell the story in your own words, using as much German as you can, to a parent, friend or one of your brothers and sisters. Don't worry if you can't remember every word. Do the best you can, and review the audio if you need to.
For an even greater challenge, write the next chapter for each diglot weave. If the story hadn't ended, what would happen next?

The Three Bears I

(Review Questions)

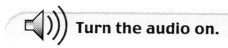 **Turn the audio on.**

Track 10

Narrator: Even though you are pretty sure the clue is in the west wing of the Schönbrunn Schloss, there is still a large area that you need to search. You break up to search more quickly, but it is almost noon when you come back together. You have been fascinated by all of the beautiful objects in the rooms, but you are beginning to lose hope of finding the clue.

Tony: What if Nikolaus has already found the clue, Onkel Otto?

Otto: Let's hope he hasn't. For right now, though, let's go down to the café and get some lunch. I don't know about you young people, but I could use a rest.

Narrator: You realize that you are starving, and you're very glad to get something to eat. In the café, your Onkel orders some tasty sandwiches for all of you, and then for dessert you get Black Forest cake, a delicious chocolate cake with cherries and whipped cream. If you would like to make Black Forest Cake, there is a recipe in the back of your workbook. While finishing your dessert, you and your Onkel discuss what to do next.

Margarethe: Do you know the story well enough to know what to look for?

Lisa: I think so.

Note: Review questions are audio only.

 Turn the audio off.

The Three Bears II
(Diglot Weave)

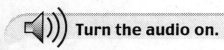 **Turn the audio on.**

Tony: I'm beginning to think that the clue isn't in the west wing, Onkel Otto.

Lisa: Me too. If it were, Nikolaus would have found it already.

Margarethe: Think, Vater. Was there anywhere else mentioned in the memoirs where Herr Trapp spent a lot of time?

Otto: Let me see… I think the only other place he mentions is the gardens.

Tony: Let's go out there and see what we can find.

Narrator: You are all glad to get out of the cool darkness of the Schloss and into the bright, warm sunlight outside. The gardens are beautiful here, full of mazes and flowers. There are even topiaries, trees grown and cut to look like statues of animals. You pass one garden of colorful, bushy flowers. The flowers are almost completely covered in colorful butterflies, with many more flying around nearby.

Otto: Those flowers are called butterfly bushes. They attract the butterflies.

Tony: Well, there are your freely flying butterflies, Lisa.

Lisa: Sie sind so schön!

Otto: It's a pity we don't have more time to look at them, but we need to find that next clue. Let's check the maze.

Narrator: You begin to wind your way through the maze, but the hedges are so high that you cannot see where you are going. You twist and turn and always seem to come up against a dead end.

Margarethe: This is pretty difficult, Vater. I have an idea. While we are trying to get out, why don't you tell us the second version of the story? That way the children will be sure to know all of the words.

Otto: That's a good idea, Margarethe. Listen carefully, Tony and Lisa.

Die geschichte von Goldlöchen und die drei Bären

Here is the next level of der berühmten Geschichte about die drei Bären und das kleine Mädchen named Goldilocks. In German her Name ist Goldlöchen.

As in other children's stories, diese Geschichte begins with the words: Es war einmal. Now hör zu.

Es waren einmal drei Bären. They lived in einem Haus im Wald. If you remember the first version of diese Geschichte, you know what ein Haus is und what der Wald is. Ein Wald ist where die Wölfe und die Bären and other Tiere live, right? Die drei Bären are der Vatibär, die Muttibärin, und das Babybärchen. One morning die Muttibärin cooked up a pot of oatmeal Brei. Then she set der Tisch with drei Schüssel und drei Löffel; eine große Schüssel und ein großer Löffel für den Vatibären, ein mittelgroße Schüssel und ein mittelgroße Löffel for herself, und eine kleine Schüssel und ein kleine Löffel für das Baby-bärchen. She filled die drei Schüsseln with the hot Brei and called out, "Vatibär, Babybärchen, kommt und esst!"

Der Vatibär sat down at den Tisch, picked up his großen Löffel und tasted den Brei in seiner großen Schüssel. "Mensch! Too hot, der Brei is too hieß," sagte er.

Die Muttibärin sat down at den Tisch, picked up her mittelgroßen Löffel, und tasted den Brei in ihrer mittelgroßen Schüssel. "Auha! Ja, der Brei ist zu heiß," sagte sie.

Das Babybärchen sat down at den Tisch, picked up seinen kleinen Löffel, und tasted den Brei. "Auah! Zu heiß, der Brei ist is zu heiß," sagte er.

Then der Vatibär sagte, "I say, let's take a walk im Wald."

Die Muttibärin sagte, "Oh yes, let's take einen Spaziergang im Wald."

Das Babybärchen sagte, "Ja, gehen wir im Wald spazieren."

Then der Vatibär, die Muttibärin, und das Babybärchen went out spazieren zu gehen im Wald. Aber they forgot to lock die Tür.

Now, while die drei Bären were taking einen Spaziergang im Wald, ein kleines Mädchen came by. It was Goldlöchen. She saw das Haus der drei Bären. She didn't know that it was das Haus der drei Bären. She knocked on die Tür. No one came an die Tür. She opened die Tür und sagte, "You-hoo!" No one answered. So she entered ins Haus.

First she went into die Küche. There she saw die drei Schüsseln auf dem Tisch. "I'm hungry," sagte sie. "Ich habe Hunger. I think no one will mind if I probeire this Brei ."

Then Goldlöchen sat down at den Tisch, picked up dem großen Löffel, und probierte den Brei in der großen Schüssel, der Schüssel des Vatibären. "Auah! Dieser Brei ist zu heiß!" sagte sie.

Then she went over and picked up den mittelgroßen Löffel und probierte den Brei in der mittelgroßen Schüssel, der Schüssel der Muttibärin. "Auah!" sagte sie. "Dieser Brei ist zu heiß, too!"

Then she went over and picked dem kleinen Löffel, und probierte den Brei in der Schüssel des Babybärchens. "Aaaah!" she said, "dieser Brei ist just right." And without thinking, Goldlöchen ate it all up . . .sie aß alles auf.

Then she went into the living room...das Wohnzimmer. There she sah drei Stühle: einen großen Stuhl, den Stuhl des Vatibären; einen mittelgroßen Stuhl, den Stuhl der Muttibärin; und einen klein Stuhl, den Stuhl des Babybärchens.

First Goldlöchen sitzte sich auf den großen Stuhl. "Auah! Dieser Stuhl ist zu hart," sagte sie.

Then she went over und sitzte sich auf den mittelgroßen Stuhl. "Oh! Dieser Stuhl ist zu weich," sagte sie.

Then she went over und sitzte auf den klein Stuhl. "Aaaah! Dieser Stuhl ist just right," sagte sie. As she leaned back, der Stuhl broke.

She picked herself up and went upstairs to das Schlafzimmer. There she sah drei Betten: ein großes Bett, das Bett des Vatibären; ein mittelgroßes Bett, das Bett der Muttibärin; und ein kleines Bett, das Bett des Babybärchens.
First Goldlöchen legte sich auf das großes Bett, das Bett des Vatibären. "Auah! Dieses Bett ist zu hart!" sagte sie.
Then she went over und legte sich auf das mittelgroßes Bett. "Oh! Dieses Bett ist zu weich!" sagte sie.

Then she went over und legte sich auf das kleine Bett. "Aaaah!, Dieses Bett ist just right," sagte sie. Then she put her head on the pillow and soon schlief ein. Just then die drei Bären returned from their Spaziergang im Wald. First they went into die Küche. There der Vatibär sah seine Schüssel und sagte, "Oh-oh, somebody has tasted meinen Brei."

Die Muttibärin sah ihre Schüssel und sagte, "Oh-oh, jemand has tasted *meinen Brei probierte, too."*

Das Babybärchen sah seine Schüssel und sagte, "Oh, jemand hat meinen Brei, too, und sie aß alles auf." Und das Babybärchen began to cry.

Then die drei Bären went into das Wohnzimmer. Der Vatibär looked at seinen großen Stuhl und brüllte, "Someone has sat auf meinen Stuhl."
Die Muttibärin sah ihren mittelgroßen Stuhl und sagte, "Jemand has sat auf meinen Stuhl, too."

Das Babybärchen sah seinen kleinene Stuhl und sagte, "Jemand hat auf meinen Stuhl geseßan, too, und hat ihn serbrochen!" Und das Babybärchen began to weinen.

Then die drei Bären went upstairs. Der Vatibär looked at sein großes Bett und brüllte, "Jemand has lain in meinem Bett."
Die Muttibärin sah ihr mittelgroßes Bett und sagte, "Jemand hat auch in meinem Bett gelegen."

Das Babybärchen sah sein kleines Bett und sagte, "Jemand hat in meinem Bett gelegen, UND HIER IST SIE!"

Hearing this, Goldlöchen wachte auf. Seeing die Bären, sie schrie, "AAAAAH!" She jumped out of dem Bett und lief nach Hause.
And she never returned to dem Haus der drei Bären again.

 Turn the audio off.

Performance Challenge:
There are four parts to this Performance Challenge:
1. Read the story silently to yourself.
2. Read the story aloud to yourself.
3. Read the story aloud to a parent, friend or one of your brothers and sisters.
4. Retell the story in your own words, using as much German as you can, to a parent, friend or one of your brothers and sisters. Don't worry if you can't remember every word. Do the best you can, and review the audio if you need to.
For an even greater challenge, write the next chapter for each diglot weave. If the story hadn't ended, what would happen next?

The Three Bears II

(Story Telling)

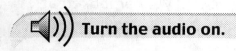 **Turn the audio on.**

Track 13

Narrator: You finally find the center of the maze, which is filled with ponds and peacocks. You also see several Gänse swimming lazily in the ponds. You search the area but do not see any Bären. Still, you are pleased to sit and rest in the shade for a moment.

Tony: These gardens are amazing. They're the perfect place to hide something. I'm sure the clue is hidden in here somewhere.

Lisa: I agree, and I still think we have a good chance at finding those manuscripts before Nikolaus does. We haven't seen him in the garden, so he probably hasn't thought of looking out here.

Otto: Well, that's true, Lisa, but you can't forget that Nikolaus has two large advantages over us. Erstens, he has Herr Trapp's memoirs. Zweitens, he speaks German fluently, while both of you are still learning.

Tony: Ja, but we're understanding more and more as we go along.

Otto: Are you? Did you feel like you understood the story I told you?

Lisa: Yes, I think we did.

Otto: Okay, then, I'd like you to retell the story back to me, using as much German as you can. Are you ready?

Now retell the story, using as much German as you can.

 Turn the audio off.

Word Puzzle 1

(The Three Bears)

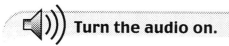 **Turn the audio on.**

Track 14

Narrator: Convinced that the clue is not in the maze, you thread your way out, which does not take near as long as finding your way in, but you are surprised to find yourself coming out of a different exit than before. This one leads into a topiary garden.

Lisa: Tony! Look at that!

Tony: Look, Onkel Otto! I wonder if that is where the next clue is.

Otto: It's possible. Let's look around.

Narrator: You begin to search the garden, when three topiaries catch your attention.

Lisa: Tony, do you see that?

Tony: Those bushes are cut to look like three bears, a Mutter, Vater, and baby. And they're bushes, so of course they're growing. That must be where the clue is hidden!

Narrator: Excited, you run up to the topiaries. Buried just below the surface in the baby bear's shade is the next piece of parchment, which has a puzzle on it.

Lisa: Onkel Otto! Come and see what we found.

Otto: Good work, children. This puzzle looks quite difficult, though. Are you sure you know the words from the story well enough to solve it?

Tony: I think we do.

Narrator: You begin walking back to your car, the puzzle in hand.

Otto: Well, children, if you know all the words you need, then perhaps you should try to solve the puzzle.

Lisa: I'm ready. Let's try!

Tony: Ja. Let's take a look.

 Turn the audio off.

Fill in the blanks in the puzzle below by following the numbered clues. The letters that fall in the circled blanks will make additional words that will help you on your adventure.

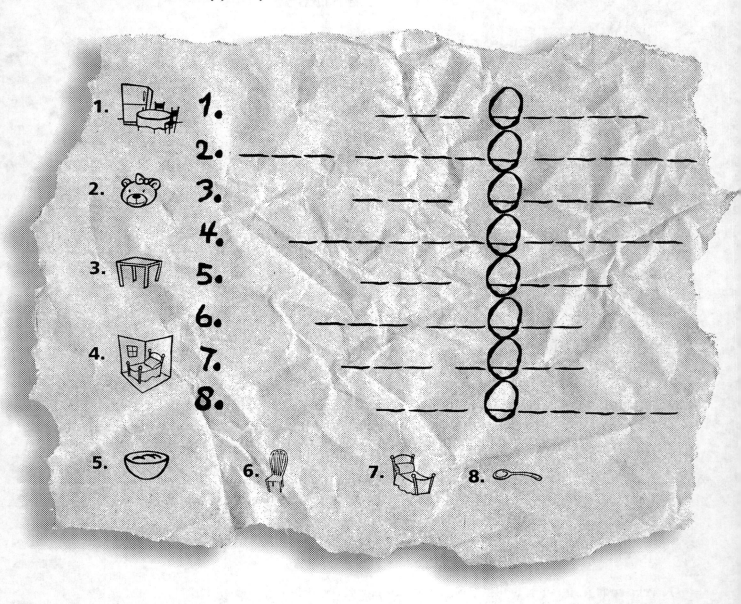

The Dog, the Cat, and the Mouse I
(Diglot Weave)

 **Turn the audio on.**

Track 15

Narrator: The next morning, you wake up to see your Onkel Otto packing your bags.

Tony: Are we going to find the next clue?

Otto: Yes. The puzzle we found yesterday evening said "Kitzbühl", which is a city up in the Alps. That's where we're going next.

Narrator: Excited to be on your way, you help your Onkel pack up all your things and you pile into the car.

Margarethe: Aber, Vater, how will we be able to find one clue in the whole city?

Otto: That's a good question, Margarethe. I was looking through my folklore research last night and I found a story that Herr Trapp associated with Kitzbühl. I think that it will help us find the next clue.

Lisa: Great. Can we hear it?

Otto: Sure. Listen carefully. It's okay if you don't know all the words yet.

Die geschichte von Hund, Katze und Maus

Track 16

Eine Maus, eine Katze, und ein Hund wohen together under the same *Dach in Deutschland.* They live *in einem Haus* like *das Haus in dem du wohnst.* Even though *die Tiere sprechen andere* languages, *die Katze und der Hund sind gute Freunde.*

Aber die Katze ist kein Freund mit der Maus. Die Katze ist der Feind nummer Eins. Wenn die Katze die Maus sieht, sie tries to *sie zu fangen. Sie* wants to *sie essen, aber die Maus entkommt* always. *Die Maus* runs to her *loch in der Wand unter dem Herd.*

There inside *dem Loch in der Wand unter dem Herd ist* wo *die Maus wohnt. Es ist bequem und safe* there. *Die Katze* can squeeze *unter dem Herd, aber sie ist zu groß in das Loch zu gehen,* wo *die Maus entkommt wenn die Katze* tries to *sie fangen.*

Die Maus schläft am Tag, aber um Mitternacht, wenn es dark ist, und wenn die ganze Welt schläft, und wenn alles ruhig ist, die Maus leaves *ihr Loch und sucht* essen *in der Küche. Sie* looks *in alle Richtungen,* sniffing *etwas zu essen, some stück essen, das jemand* has left out or dropped *auf dem Boden.* Best of all *ist* when she can *Käse riechen, besonders Schweizer Käse, aber sie frißt* any *Käse. In der Nacht, as* much as she likes to essen in der Küche suchen, sie always has to watch out for die Katze.

She doesn't have to watch out auf den Hund, denn der Hund ist ihr Freund. Even though they andere Sprachen sprechen, sie sind gute Freunde. Sie sind such gute Freunde, dass manchmal, wenn der Hund wakes up um Mitternacht und wants to play, er goes in doe Küche, sticks seine Nase unter dem Herd, und bellt softly, "arf, arf," Freunde kommt spielen and play. Und die Maus, knowing dass she is safe mit dem Hund, verläßt ihr Loch und läuft überall in dem Haus while everyone else schläft.

Eines Nachts hört die Maus to make sure dass no one was awake und dass sie could sihr Loch verlaßen und something zu essen suchen. Suddenly sie hört a faint sound outside von seinem Loch: "arf, arf." "Oh," sie glaubt, "Es ist mein Freund, der Hund. Ich werde hin aus gehen und mit ihm spielen." Excited, lief sie aus seinem Loch, und die Katze fing sie mit ihren sharp claws. Die Katze, die die Maus by dem Schwanz ge fangen hatte, saw him und sagte, "arf, arf."

Now you see how useful it is to another Sprache lernen.

Die arme Maus thought, "If only I knew wie zu sprechen like ein Löwen oder ein Hund, die Katze would be scared und I could entkommen." But die Maus didn't know die Sprache der Löwen, nor die Sprache der Hunde. Sie konnte nur die Sprache der Mäuse.

Das only thing dass sie could sagen before the end came was, "quiek, quiek."

 Turn the audio off.

Performance Challenge:

There are four parts to this Performance Challenge:
1. Read the story silently to yourself.
2. Read the story aloud to yourself.
3. Read the story aloud to a parent, friend or one of your brothers and sisters.
4. Retell the story in your own words, using as much German as you can, to a parent, friend or one of your brothers and sisters. Don't worry if you can't remember every word. Do the best you can, and review the audio if you need to.
For an even greater challenge, write the next chapter for each diglot weave. If the story hadn't ended, what would happen next?

The Dog, the Cat, and the Mouse I

(Scatter Chart)

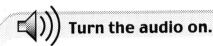 **Turn the audio on.**

Track 17

Narrator: You arrive at Kitzbühl and are charmed with the beauty of the little town. The town is surrounded by an old stone wall that was built hundreds of years ago. The streets are lined with tall wooden houses with sharp pointed roofs that look like shadows of the jagged Alps above them.

Margarethe: I remember we came here once for vacation when I was younger, and we went hiking up in the Alps.

Otto: Well, we're going hiking again. Herr Trapp had a cabin up here in the mountains, the Bergen, where I think the next clue may be hidden. First, though, let's go and find somewhere to spend the night.

Narrator: Your Onkel finds a charming little inn, just as dark is falling. You are lying in bed, almost ready to fall asleep, when he comes to say goodnight.

Tony: Do you think we'll be able to find the clue tomorrow, Onkel Otto?

Otto: I hope so. I've been up there before, so it shouldn't be too hard to find, but the hike is very long and tiring. Try to get some rest.

Lisa: I'm excited to find the next clue, but I'm not sure I understood all the words in the story.

Otto: Okay, well, while you're getting ready to go to sleep, we can go over some of the words together.

Track 18

Look at the pictures on your workbook page and point to what you hear.

der Moden
the floor

sucht
searches

der Herd
the stove

Mitternacht
midnight

die Wand
the wall

das Loch
the hole

Gute Freunde
good friends

das Dach
the roof

riechen
to smell

fangen
to trap

 Turn the audio off.

The Dog, the Cat, and the Mouse II
(Diglot Weave)

Your Onkel wakes you before sunrise the next morning. In the pale gray semidarkness, you get ready for your hike into the Alps, die Alpen. The morning is clear but slightly cold, and your Onkel makes sure you all have gloves and scarves. He explains that it will be colder up in the mountains, even if the hiking does warm you. After a breakfast of warm porridge and sausages, you drive up towards the mountains. When you have driven to the base of the trail, your Onkel parks the car and you all climb out. The sky is getting lighter, and you can see the jagged peaks of die Alpen highlighted against it.

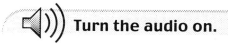 **Turn the audio on.**

Track 19

Tony: Wow. The view from here is amazing.

Margarethe: Isn't it? Die Alpen are some of the tallest and most beautiful Bergen in the world.

Narrator: You all begin your hike up the steep trail that winds through the rocks and brush of the mountain. As you walk, you see more and more snow and ice.

Tony: Are we going all the way to the top, Onkel Otto?

Otto: Nein, there is a small pond just over a mile farther where Herr Trapp built his cabin. That's where we'll stop.

Lisa: While we're heading up, will you tell us the full version of the story so that we know what to look for?

Otto: That's a good idea, and it will take your minds off the cold. Listen carefully.

Die geschichte von Hund, Katze und Maus

Track 20

Ein Maus, eine Katze, und ein Hund wohnen unter dem selben Dach in Deutschland. Es ist ein Haus wie das Haus indem du wohnst. Obwohl die Tiere veschiedene Sprachen sprechen sind, die Katze und der Hund sehr gute Freunde. Aber die Katze und der Maus sind keine Freunde. Die Katze ist der Feind nummer Eins. Wenn die Katze die Maus sieht, versucht sie, sie zu fangen. Sie will sie essen, aber die Maus entkommt immer; die Maus lauft in ihr Loch in der Wand unter dem Herd.

Die Maus wohnt in dem Loch unter dem Herd. Dort ist es bequem und sicher. Die Katze kann unter dem Herd umreichen, aber sie ist zu groß in das Loch zu gehen, wo die Maus immer entkommt wenn die Katze versucht sie zu fangen. Die Maus schläft am Tag, aber um Mitternacht, wenn es dunkel ist und die ganze Welt schläft, und wenn alles ruhig ist, geht die Maus aus ihrem Loch und sucht essen in der Küche. Sie schaut in alle Richtungen, sniffing etwas zu essen, ein Stück Essen das jemand auf den Boden fallen lassen hat. Das Beste ist wenn sie Käse riechen kann, besonders Schweizer Käse, aber sie frißt jeden Käse. Bei Nacht, obwohl sie gern Essen in der Küche sucht, muß sie immer auf die Katze aufpassen. Sei braucht nicht auf den Hund auf zu passen, denn der Hund ist ihr Freund. Obwohl sie andere Sprachen sprechen, sie sind gute Freunde. Sie sind solch gute Freunde dass manchmal, wenn der hund um Mitternacht aufwacht und spielen will, er seine Nase unter dem Herd steckt und leise bellt, "arf, arf!" Freunde kommt spielen. Die Maus, wissend dass sie sicher mit dem Hund ist, verlaßt ihr Loch und läuft überall in dem Haus, während dieganze Welt schläft.

Eines Nachts, hört sich die Maus sehr gut um, um sicher zu stellen dass niemand wach ist und dass sie ihr Loch verlaßen kann und etwas zu essen zu suchen. Plötzlich, hört sie ein leise geroch draußen vor ihrem Loch, "arf, arf." "Oh," glaubt die Maus, "es ist mein Freund, der Hund. Ich werde hin aus gehen und mit ihm spielen." Schnell, verlaßt die Maus ihr Loch, und die Katze fängt sie mit ihren scharfe Kralle. Die Katze, mit die Mausby dem Schwanz gefangen hatte, sieht sie und sagte, "arf, arf."

Nun verstehst du wie wichtig es ist, eine andere Sprache zu sprechen.

Die arme Maus glaubt, "Wenn ich nur wie ein Löwen oder ein Hund sprechen könnte, hätte die Katze Angst, und ich könnte entkommen." Aber die Maus kann nicht die Sprache des Löwens, noch de Sprache des Hundes. Sie kann nur die Sprache der Mäuse.

Das einzige was die Maus vor dem Ende sagen konnte war, "quiek, quiek."

 Turn the audio off.

Performance Challenge:

There are four parts to this Performance Challenge:
1. Read the story silently to yourself.
2. Read the story aloud to yourself.
3. Read the story aloud to a parent, friend or one of your brothers and sisters.
4. Retell the story in your own words, using as much German as you can, to a parent, friend or one of your brothers and sisters.
Don't worry if you can't remember every word. Do the best you can, and review the audio if you need to.
For an even greater challenge, write the next chapter for each diglot weave. If the story hadn't ended, what would happen next?

The Dog, the Cat, and the Mouse II

(Story Telling)

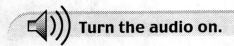 **Turn the audio on.**

Narrator: The sun has risen by the time you reach the lake, and you are grateful for the warmth. Your Onkel points out the cabin that Herr Trapp built, which is now reduced to a stone shell.

Lisa: It looks ruined, Onkel Otto. Do you think we'll still be able to find the next clue?

Otto: I hope so. It should still be here, unless Nikolaus has found it before us.

Tony: How could he? He didn't find the clue at the Schönbrunn, we did.

Otto: True, and that gave us a big head start. Nikolaus still has the memoirs, though, and Herr Trapp may have copied the clue in there as well.

Tony: Oh.

Margarethe: Don't be discouraged, we'll just have to find the next clue first.

Tony: How will we know where to look, Onkel Otto?

Otto: Well, if I remember the clue from the memoirs, it was "Such den Feind der Maus." Do you remember the story well enough to figure out that clue?

Lisa: Ich glaube schon.

Otto: Just to make sure, I'd like you to tell the story back to me, using as much German as you can. Remember to look for things that have to do with the clue.

 Turn the audio off.

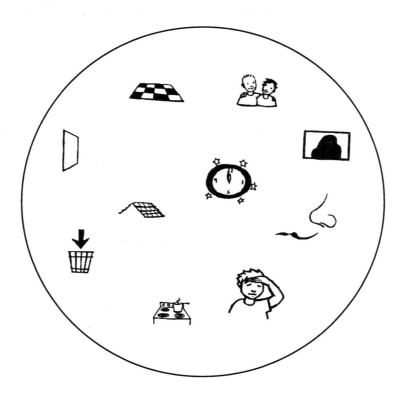

 Turn the audio off.

Word Puzzle 2

(The Dog, the Cat, and the Mouse)

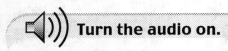 **Turn the audio on.**

Track 22

Tony: So, the Hund was the Freund of the Maus…

Lisa: And the Katze was the Feind.

Tony: Right! We need to find a Katze.

Margarethe: Gute Arbeit, Kinder! Let's start looking.

Narrator: You begin to search through the rubble of the cabin, keeping your eye out for a Katze. After awhile, Margarethe and Onkel Otto go outside to search in the gardens.

Lisa: I'm not seeing anything that looks like a cat… how about you?

Tony: No… wait a minute! Look at that!

Narrator: Next to the crumbling doorway, you see two stone figures on either side. On the left side is a dog, and on the right side is a cat.

Lisa: It must be on the cat somewhere! Let's look.

Narrator: Carefully, you feel around the stonecat, and after a moment, you realize that you can slide it off, revealing a hollow underneath in the floor. Inside are two pieces of parchment. You pick the first one up.

Tony: This looks like a map. Look, though, it's ripped, I can't tell what it is.

Lisa: What's on the second piece of parchment?

Tony: Let me see… Yes! This looks like the next clue!

Lisa: It's another puzzle. Let's go show Onkel Otto.

Narrator: You run outside and show your Onkel the clue. He is very excited, and you all sit down to solve it together.

 Turn the audio off.

Fill in the blanks in the puzzle below by following the numbered clues. The letters that fall in the circled blanks will make additional words that will help you on your adventure.

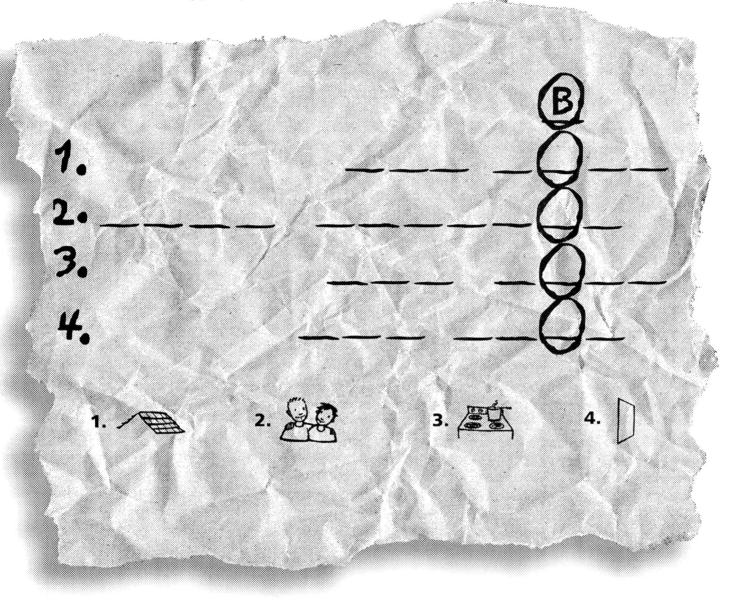

Hard Days

(Horseshoe Story)

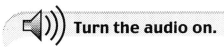 **Turn the audio on.**

Track 23

Otto: "Baden." I know that, it's a town over near the border to Germany.

Margarethe: That must be where the next clue is. Let's go.

Lisa: Just a minute. Tony and I should go back to the cabin to make sure we put that cat back.

Narrator: Quickly, you both run over to the cabin. When you come near it, however, you slow down, because you hear a voice inside.

Nikolaus: Ach nein, man hat die Katze…jemand hat den Hinweis!

Tony: Who is that?

Lisa: I don't know…it might be Nikolaus!

Narrator: Worried, you run back to your Onkel and tell him what you heard.

Otto: I think you're right, Lisa. Nikolaus must be here looking for the next clue. Let's hurry, he mustn't find us here.

Narrator: You all rush down the mountain as fast as you can.

Margarethe: How will we know where to find the next clue in Baden, Vater?

Otto: Well, I remember from my research a story that had to do with the time Herr Trapp spent there. I can tell it to you while we get to our car. Listen closely.

Tough Days for my Little Brother

1 Vor drei Tagen…fiel mein Bruder und brach sich den Arm.

2 Vor gestern…schnitt er sich unabsichtlich mit dem Messer.

3 Gestern…verbrannte er sich die Hand.

4 Heute…wurde er Krank und ohnmächtig.

5 Morgen…geht er zum Arzt hoffe ich.

6 Übermorgen…hoffe ich, geht er ins Krankenhaus.

7 In drei Tagen…hoffe ich, wird es ihn besser gehen.

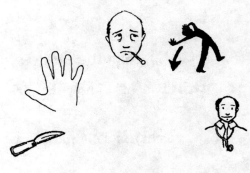

Turn the audio off.

Performance Challenge:

Create hand actions to represent the actions in the horseshoe story. (For example: Make up different actions to represent the animals you heard about in the story.) After you have created the actions, perform your mini-play for a parent, friend, or one of your bothers and sisters. Remember to narrate your actions in German and then translate your words if your audience does not understand German. For an even greater challenge, try writing your own horseshoe story. Choose several things or people that are related to each other in some way. Think of a chain of events that connects the characters in the story. To finish the story, figure out how the events could be reversed in order to back through the pictures and the plot.

Hard Days
(Scatter Chart)

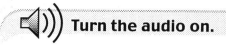 **Turn the audio on.**

Track 25

Narrator: You arrive at Baden just before nightfall.

Lisa: Why would Trapp come to Baden, Onkel Otto? It seems out of the way.

Otto: Well, Herr Trapp was a trickster. He liked to come here because of the hot springs. The rich people of Deutschland and Österreich would come and bathe here because they thought the springs were healthy, and he would play his terrible tricks on them.

Tony: Hot springs?

Otto: Yes, Tony. The water gets heated from the inside of the earth, then comes pouring out, boiling hot. It was very popular here, because of the cold winters. Everyone would come and bathe.

Narrator: You try to imagine this as you check into your hotel room.

Margarethe: Good night, Tony, Lisa. We'll try to find the next clue tomorrow.

Lisa: I'm not sure how well I understood the story, Margarethe. We might have trouble finding the clue.

Otto: Well, why don't we go over some of the words while you get ready for bed? Hört gut zu carefully.

Look at the pictures on your workbook page and point to what you hear.

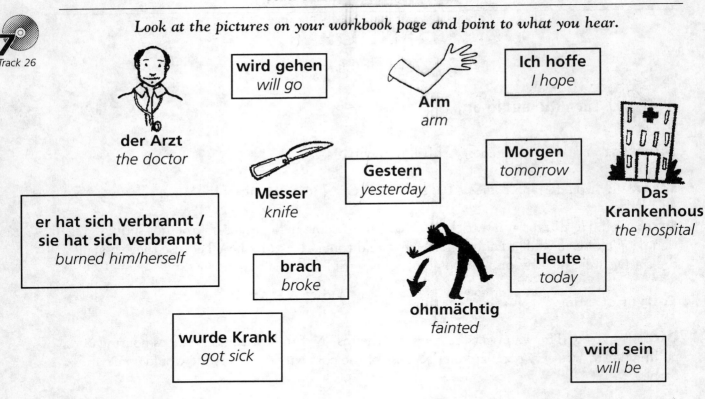

der Arzt
the doctor

wird gehen
will go

Arm
arm

Ich hoffe
I hope

Messer
knife

Gestern
yesterday

Morgen
tomorrow

Das Krankenhous
the hospital

**er hat sich verbrannt /
sie hat sich verbrannt**
burned him/herself

brach
broke

ohnmächtig
fainted

Heute
today

wurde Krank
got sick

wird sein
will be

🔊 **Turn the audio off.**

Performance Challenge:

Choose five of the new words and pictures that you learned in the Scatter Chart. Show the pictures to a parent, friend, or one of your brothers and sisters and explain to them how you think the picture represents the words you have learned. For an even greater challenge, create your own story using the pictures. Bring out the artist in yourself by drawing your own versions of the pictographs and making a book with the story you create.

Mystery Maps

(Austria)

 **Turn the audio on.**

Track 27

Narrator: The next day, you go to visit the hot springs, hoping to find the next clue. The nearer you get, the worse it smells.

Tony: Whew! It smells like rotten eggs in here.

Otto: That's the sulfur in the springs, Tony.

Lisa: How could people bear to soak in the water?

Margarethe: That's a good question, but people still do.

Narrator: You pull your shirt collar up over your nose to try and block out the smell, and then begin to look around.

Tony: What exactly are we looking for, Onkel Otto?

Otto: Well, there was an old bathhouse around here somewhere that was Herr Trapp's favorite place for pranks. It was called "Schwere Tage", you see, and so he liked it.

Lisa: There! Doesn't that sign say "Schwere Tage", Onkel Otto?

Otto: Yes, it does. That must be the place. Let's go inside and look.

Narrator: You head inside the bathhouse, and begin to search. The house is built of old limestone, and there is a fireplace over in the corner.

Tony: Hey, what about the fireplace? In the story, he "verbrennt sich seine Hand", right?

Otto: Good thinking, Tony! Let's see.

Narrator: You go over to the fireplace and find a loose stone. You pry it up, and underneath, you see another piece of parchment.

Lisa: What is it?

Tony: It looks like a map… wait! Do we still have that half of a map from before? I think they fit together. And look! There are clues written on the side.

Otto: Well, let's see if we can figure out what this means.

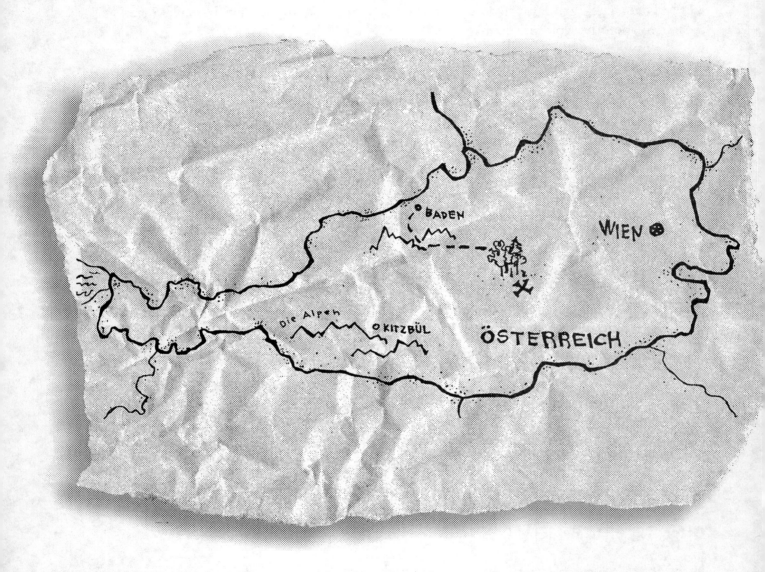

Manuscripts!

(Success)

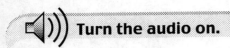 **Turn the audio on.**

Narrator: Having found the map, you quickly leave the bathhouse and head to your car.

Otto: Let's see if we can find this place on the map. It shouldn't be too far out of town.

Nikolaus: Entschuldigen sie, ich suche…

Lisa: Look, over there! Isn't that Nikolaus?

Otto: You're right! Let's go.

Narrator: It's too late, however. Nikolaus has seen you and begins to run over.

Margarethe: Schnell! Ins Auto!

Narrator: You all pile into the car and drive away as fast as you can.

Nikolaus: Halten sie an!

Narrator: Deciding that you have no time to spare, you immediately begin your search for the next clue. The map leads you out of town and into the mountains, where you drive until you find an old trail leading through the woods.

Otto: This must be the right place. Let's go on foot from here.

Narrator: You all clamber out of the car and begin to search through the woods. It's getting late, however, and darker.

Lisa: We'll never find the manuscripts if the sun goes down. It'll be too hard to look.

Narrator: Just then, however, you see an old fallen log lying near the path. You wouldn't have noticed it, except that carved into the log, so deeply that it still shows despite all the moss and lichens, is a large "X."

Tony: This must be it! Quick, let's move it.

Narrator: You all push on the log together, and slowly it gives way until you can reach underneath. Beneath the log, in a small, muddy hollow, is an old, worn brown leather portfolio. Your Onkel picks it up and opens it. Inside are yellowed old papers, filled with musical notes written in black ink.

Lisa: That's it!

Tony: We found the manuscripts!

 Turn the audio off.

Test 1

(*Review*)

 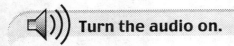

Narrator: It is one week later, and you are sitting in your Onkel's living room in Germany, where your adventure began. The manuscripts have been returned to a German Museum, a lost treasure to the entire country. Your parents have flown in to celebrate with you. Just then, however, your Onkel comes in, and he looks very unhappy.

Margarethe: Vater! What's wrong?

Otto: Something terrible has happened, Margarethe. Nikolaus has pulled off a heist worthy of Herr Trapp himself.

Lisa: What do you mean, Onkel Otto?

Otto: Nikolaus has broken into the museum and stolen the manuscripts. They are now in his possession.

Tony: This is terrible! We need to get them back!

Otto: Yes, we do, but I cannot take you children with me. Nikolaus has fled the country. Luckily, he left with his cousin, Hans. Hans is an old friend of mine and called me to warn me. Nikolaus has gone to Luxembourg. He is now a criminal on the run, and following him is far too dangerous for you children.

Lisa: But, Onkel Otto, we can help you!

Tony: Yeah, our German is getting besser!

Otto: Well, that's true, but…

Lisa: Please let us go with you, Onkel Otto!

Narrator: Your Onkel goes and talks it over with your parents. Finally, they agree that if you can show how much German you have learned, they will let you go to Luxembourg with your Onkel.

Test 1

Track 30

◁))) Turn the audio on.

A. Frame Identifications

For each question, you will see a box with pictures. You will hear a statement about one of the pictures. There will be a pause of 10 seconds to identify the picture, and then the statement will be repeated.

1.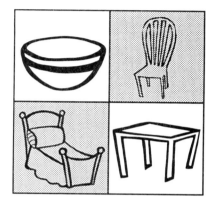

2.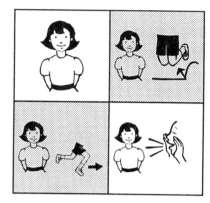

3.

4.

5.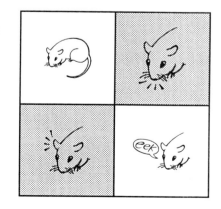

Comprehension Multiple-Choice

Complete the following conversations by choosing the correct answer from the options listed.

1. "Jeder hat Hunger."

    A. Gehen wir spazieren im Wald.

    B. Sehr Gut, danke.

    C. Essen wir.

    D. Ja, er is sehr klug.

2. Who owned den mittelgroßen stuhl?

    A. die Muttibärin

    B. der Vatibär

    C. das Babybärchen

    D. Goldilocken

3. What was wrong with dem Brei des Vatibären?

    A. zu weich

    B zu klein

    C. zu hart

    D. zu heiß

4. Why did die Maus come out um Mitternacht?

    A. um mit der Katze zu spielen

    B. um etwas zu essen zu suchen

    C. um in der Küche zu schlafen

    D. um in das Loch hineinzugehen

5. Wann wird dein Bruder zum Arzt gehen?

    A. vor drei Tagen

    B. vorgestern

    C. gestern

    D. in zwei oder drei Tagen

Now go on to complete the reading/writing portion of this test.

 Turn the audio off.

Matching

Choose the statements that match and draw a line to connect the two.

1. bed	a. der Löffel
2. stove	b. der Stuhl
3. chair	c. das Bett
4. bowl	d. der Herd
5. spoon	e. der Schlüssel

True or False

Write T or F for each statement.

_____ 1. Die drei Bären haben Goldilocken mit Milch, für Frühstück gegessen.

_____ 2. Es war ein Unfall daß Goldilocken den Stuhl kaputt gemacht hat.

_____ 3. Die Katze hat einen Witz mit der Maus gespielt.

_____ 4. Der Hund war ein guter Freund von der Maus.

_____ 5. Die Maus hat Käse gern gegessen.

Answer Key

1.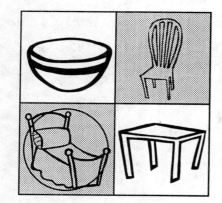

2.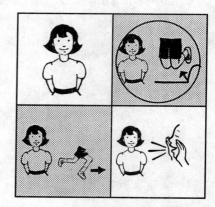

3.

4.

5.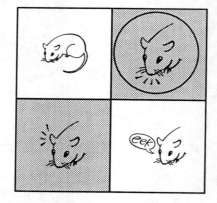

Comprehension Multiple-Choice

1. C.

2. A.

3. D.

4. B.

5. D.

Matching

1. C

2. D

3. B

4. E

5. A

True or False

1. F

2. T

3. T

4. T

5. T

The Adventure Continues

(Luxembourg)

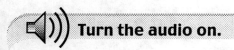 **Turn the audio on.**

Track 1

Narrator: You and your Onkel Otto step off of the plane that has brought you safely to Luxembourg. You are so excited that he has agreed to take you with him to search for Nikolaus and his cousin Hans!

Tony: Hey, look at that sign over there. The first part is in German, but I don't recognize the rest of the words.

Otto: That's because there are three national languages here in Luxembourg, Tony. The first is German, which we will be speaking. The second is French, and the third is a native language called Luxembourgish. Even though Luxembourg is the smallest country in Europe, it still has a very diverse culture.

Lisa: What city will we be going to first to find Nikolaus, Onkel Otto?

Otto: We'll be here in Luxembourg first. The whole country is known as the Grand Duchy of Luxembourg, but when people talk about "Luxembourg" they generally mean the capital. Even though the whole country is smaller than Rhode Island, the smallest state in the United States, it still has the ruins of over one hundred castles in the countryside.

Lisa: Even with how small the country is, how will we ever be able to find Nikolaus?

Otto: Well, we'll need the help of Hans, and we will need to learn as much German as we can. Let's go and check into our hotel, and see what we can find out. Maybe Hans has left a note for us.

 Turn the audio off.

Wenn der Pott aber nun ein Loch hat

(Ditties)

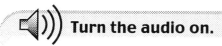 **Turn the audio on.**

Track 2

Narrator: When you arrive at your hotel, your Onkel Otto is disappointed that there has not been a note from Hans, but you are too excited by the city to mind. The city, although enormous, has retained the feeling of a very small town, with twisting cobblestone streets and tall, pointed buildings. You peer out your window, taking in the view, while your Onkel Otto finishes unpacking.

Otto: Well, Kinder, what do you think of Luxembourg?

Tony: It's amazing! I can't believe a country this small could have a city so large.

Otto: Yes, Luxembourg is very popular with tourists, especially from other European countries like France and Germany, and so the economy is mostly centered on the cities. People come here to ski or to enjoy the cuisine.

Lisa: Do you have any idea where to start looking for Nikolaus, Onkel Otto?

Otto: Well, as far as I know, Nikolaus has never been to Luxembourg before. I'm more sure of where Hans will go, as we traveled here together when we were doing some folklore research. I remember that one of Hans' favorite songs came from here.

Tony: Could you teach it to us? It might be helpful later on.

Otto: You may be right. Okay, the song is called "Wenn der Pott aber nur ein Loch hat." It's a variation of the American song "There's a whole in the bucket." Listen carefully to the first part.

Wenn der Pott aber nun ein Loch hat,
Lieber Heinrich, lieber Heinrich?
Stopf es zu, liebe, liebe Liese,
Liebe Liese, stopf 's zu!

Womit soll ich's aber zustopfen,
Lieber Heinrich, lieber Heinrich?
Mit Stroh, liebe, liebe Liese,
Liebe Liese, mit Stroh!

Let's sing that together.

Otto, Tony, Lisa:

Wenn der Pott aber nun ein Loch hat,
Lieber Heinrich, lieber Heinrich?
Stopf es zu, liebe, liebe Liese,
Liebe Liese, stopf 's zu!

Womit soll ich's aber zustopfen,
Lieber Heinrich, lieber Heinrich?
Mit Stroh, liebe, liebe Liese,
Liebe Liese, mit Stroh!

Otto: Good. Here is the second part.
Wenn das Stroh aber nun zu lang ist,
Lieber Heinrich, lieber Heinrich?
Hau es ab, liebe, liebe Liese,
Liebe Liese, hau's ab!

Womit soll ich's aber abhaun,
Lieber Heinrich, lieber Heinrich?
Mit dem Beil, liebe, liebe Liese,
Liebe Liese, mit'm Beil!
Let's sing that together.

Otto, Tony, Lisa:
Wenn das Stroh aber nun zu lang ist,
Lieber Heinrich, lieber Heinrich?
Hau es ab, liebe, liebe Liese,
Liebe Liese, hau's ab!

Womit soll ich's aber abhaun,
Lieber Heinrich, lieber Heinrich?
Mit dem Beil, liebe, liebe Liese,
Liebe Liese, mit'm Beil!

Otto: Here is the third part.
Wenn das Beil aber nun stumpf ist,
Lieber Heinrich, lieber Heinrich?
Mach es scharf, liebe, liebe Liese,
Liebe Liese, mach's scharf!

Womit soll ich's aber scharf mach'n,
Lieber Heinrich, lieber Heinrich?
Mit dem Stein, liebe, liebe Liese,
Liebe Liese, mit 'm Stein!.

Together, now.

Otto, Tony, Lisa:
Wenn das Beil aber nun stumpf ist,
Lieber Heinrich, lieber Heinrich?
Mach es scharf, liebe, liebe Liese,
Liebe Liese, mach's scharf!

Womit soll ich's aber scharf mach'n,
Lieber Heinrich, lieber Heinrich?
Mit dem Stein, liebe, liebe Liese,
Liebe Liese, mit 'm Stein!.

Otto: Excellent. Here is the next part.
Wenn der Stein aber nun zu trocken ist,
Lieber Heinrich, leiber Heinrich?
Mach ihn nass, liebe, liebe Liese,
Liebe Liese, mach ihn nass!

Womit soll ich ihn aber nass machen,
Lieber Heinrich, lieber Heinrich?
Mit dem Wasser, liebe, liebe Liese,
Liebe Liese, mit 'm Wasser!.
Now let's sing that together.

Otto, Tony, Lisa:
Wenn der Stein aber nun zu trocken ist,
Lieber Heinrich, leiber Heinrich?
Mach ihn nass, liebe, liebe Liese,
Liebe Liese, mach ihn nass!

Womit soll ich ihn aber nass machen,
Lieber Heinrich, lieber Heinrich?
Mit dem Wasser, liebe, liebe Liese,
Liebe Liese, mit 'm Wasser!.

Otto: Very good. Here is the last part.
Womit soll ich denn das Wasser holen,
Lieber Heinrich, lieber Heinrich?
Mit den Pott, liebe, liebe Liese,
Liebe Liese, mit 'm Pott!

Wenn der Pott aber nun ein Loch hat,
Lieber Heinrich, lieber Heinrich?
Lass es sein, liebe, liebe Liese,
Liebe Liese, lass es sein!.

Let's sing that part together.

Otto, Tony, Lisa:
Womit soll ich denn das Wasser holen,
Lieber Heinrich, lieber Heinrich?
Mit den Pott, liebe, liebe Liese,
Liebe Liese, mit 'm Pott!

Wenn der Pott aber nun ein Loch hat,
Lieber Heinrich, lieber Heinrich?
Lass es sein, liebe, liebe Liese,
Liebe Liese, lass es sein!.

Otto: Very good. Let's sing through the whole song now, together.

Otto, Tony, Lisa:
Wenn der Pott aber nun ein Loch hat,
Lieber Heinrich, lieber Heinrich?
Stopf es zu, liebe, liebe Liese,
Liebe Liese, stopf 's zu!

Womit soll ich's aber zustopfen,
Lieber Heinrich, lieber Heinrich?
Mit Stroh, liebe, liebe Liese,
Liebe Liese, mit Stroh!

Wenn das Stroh aber nun zu lang ist,
Lieber Heinrich, lieber Heinrich?
Hau es ab, liebe, liebe Liese,
Liebe Liese, hau's ab!

Womit soll ich's aber abhaun,
Lieber Heinrich, lieber Heinrich?
Mit dem Beil, liebe, liebe Liese,
Liebe Liese, mit'm Beil!

Wenn das Beil aber nun stumpf ist,
Lieber Heinrich, lieber Heinrich?
Mach es scharf, liebe, liebe Liese,
Liebe Liese, mach's scharf!

Womit soll ich's aber scharf mach'n,
Lieber Heinrich, lieber Heinrich?
Mit dem Stein, liebe, liebe Liese,
Liebe Liese, mit 'm Stein!

Wenn der Stein aber nun zu trocken ist,
Lieber Heinrich, leiber Heinrich?
Mach ihn nass, liebe, liebe Liese,
Liebe Liese, mach ihn nass!

Womit soll ich ihn aber nass machen,
Lieber Heinrich, lieber Heinrich?
Mit dem Wasser, liebe, liebe Liese,
Liebe Liese, mit 'm Wasser!

Womit soll ich denn das Wasser holen,
Lieber Heinrich, lieber Heinrich?
Mit den Pott, liebe, liebe Liese,
Liebe Liese, mit 'm Pott!

Wenn der Pott aber nun ein Loch hat,
Lieber Heinrich, lieber Heinrich?
Lass es sein, liebe, liebe Liese,
Liebe Liese, lass es sein!
Otto: Ausgezeichnet!

 Turn the audio off.

Performance Challenge:

Now that you have learned a new song, share your German with a parent, friend, or one of your brothers and sisters by teaching them the song. Remember to teach it in German and then translate the words into English if your partner does not understand German. For an even greater challenge, try writing a song about your culture and put it to the tune of the German song you just learned. If you need an idea to get you started, just think of what a visitor from another country would like to know about you and your family.

Bei Goldhähnchen

(Ditties)

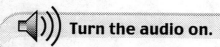 **Turn the audio on.**

Lisa: That's a funny song, Onkel Otto, but do you think it will help us find Nikolaus?

Narrator: Just then the phone rings and your Onkel Otto picks it up.

Otto: Hallo? Hallo, Hans. Wo willst du uns treflen? In Ordnung. Ich werde gleich da sein.

Tony: Was that Hans, Onkel Otto?

Otto: Yes, it was. He wants us to meet him at a small café near here where we used to eat. I'll take you there.

Narrator: You all get into your rental car and begin to drive down the street.

Otto: Hans mentioned a song that we were studying when we were here last. It is a silly song about a gold chicken. I think he meant it as a clue, but I'm not sure.

Lisa: What was the song?

Otto: It was called "Bei Goldhähnchen." The first part goes like this.

Bei Goldhähnchen war ich jüngst zu Gast,
Sie wohnen im grünen Fichtenpalast
In einem Nestchen klein,
Sehr niedlich und sehr fein!

Was hat es gegeben? Schmetterlingsei,
Mükkensalat und Grützenbrei
Und Käferbraten, famos,
Zwei Millimeter groß.
Let's sing that together.

Otto, Tony, Lisa:
Bei Goldhähnchen war ich jüngst zu Gast,
Sie wohnen im grünen Fichtenpalast
In einem Nestchen klein,
Sehr niedlich und sehr fein!

Was hat es gegeben? Schmetterlingsei,

Mükkensalat und Grützenbrei
Und Käferbraten, famos,
Zwei Millimeter groß.

Otto: Good. Here is the second part of the song.
Dann sang uns Vater Goldhähnchen was-
So zierlich klang's wie gesponnenes Glas.
Dann wurden die Kinder beseh'n,
Sehr niedlich alle zehn!

Dann sagt ich: "Leb wohl und danke sehr!"
Sie sprachen: "Bitte, wir hatten die Ehr',
Und hat uns mächtig gefreut!"
Es sind doch reizende Leut'!
Let's sing that together.

Otto, Lisa, Tony:
Dann sang uns Vater Goldhähnchen was-
So zierlich klang's wie gesponnenes Glas.
Dann wurden die Kinder beseh'n,
Sehr niedlich alle zehn!

Dann sagt ich: "Leb wohl und danke sehr!"
Sie sprachen: "Bitte, wir hatten die Ehr',
Und hat uns mächtig gefreut!"
Es sind doch reizende Leut'!

Otto: Good. Now let's sing the whole thing through.

Otto, Lisa, Tony:
Bei Goldhähnchen war ich jüngst zu Gast,
Sie wohnen im grünen Fichtenpalast
In einem Nestchen klein,
Sehr niedlich und sehr fein!

Was hat es gegeben? Schmetterlingsei,
Mükkensalat und Grützenbrei
Und Käferbraten, famos,
Zwei Millimeter groß.

Dann sang uns Vater Goldhähnchen was-
So zierlich klang's wie gesponnenes Glas.
Dann wurden die Kinder beseh'n,
Sehr niedlich alle zehn!

Dann sagt ich: "Leb wohl und danke sehr!"

Sie sprachen: "Bitte, wir hatten die Ehr',
Und hat uns mächtig gefreut!"
Es sind doch reizende Leut'!

Otto: Excellent! One more time.

Otto, Tony, Lisa:
Bei Goldhähnchen war ich jüngst zu Gast,
Sie wohnen im grünen Fichtenpalast
In einem Nestchen klein,
Sehr niedlich und sehr fein!

Was hat es gegeben? Schmetterlingsei,
Mükkensalat und Grützenbrei
Und Käferbraten, famos,
Zwei Millimeter groß.

Dann sang uns Vater Goldhähnchen was-
So zierlich klang's wie gesponnenes Glas.
Dann wurden die Kinder beseh'n,
Sehr niedlich alle zehn!

Dann sagt ich: "Leb wohl und danke sehr!"
Sie sprachen: "Bitte, wir hatten die Ehr',
Und hat uns mächtig gefreut!"
Es sind doch reizende Leut'!

Otto: Sehr gut, Kinder!

 Turn the audio off.

Performance Challenge:

Now that you have learned a new song, share your German with a parent, friend, or one of your brothers and sisters by teaching them the song. Remember to teach it in German and then translate the words into English if your partner does not understand German. For an even greater challenge, try writing a song about your culture and put it to the tune of the German song you just learned. If you need an idea to get you started, just think of what a visitor from another country would like to know about you and your family.

The Hunter and the Thief

(Match and Learn)

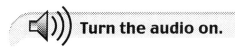 **Turn the audio on.**

Narrator: You arrive at the small café where you are supposed to meet Hans. Your Onkel Otto does not see him, so you all sit down and order something to eat while you wait. Your Onkel orders you a tasty green bean soup called La Bouneschlupp. If you would like to try and make La Bouneschlupp, there is a recipe in the back of your manual. When your Onkel goes up to pay for your meal, the waiter asks him his name, and then hands him a written note that someone left for him.

Tony: Do you think it is from Hans, Onkel Otto?

Otto: It may be. Let me see. It says, "Triff mich im Grand Ducal Schloss, wohin der Dieb geht." Hmmm. Let me see… I know what the Grand Ducal Schloss is, it's a Schloss here in Luxembourg.

Lisa: We get to go to a Schloss? Cool!

Otto: Yes, but I'm not sure what this second part means, about where the thief goes. I think it may refer to a story I remember from the research Hans and I did together.

Tony: Will you tell it to us so that we can know where to look?

Otto: First there are some words you're going to need to know. Listen carefully.

Listen to the following words and point to what you hear.

1.

die Frau the woman	*der Adler* the eagle
das Essen the food	*der Dieb* the thief

2.

das Gefängnis the prison	*die Polizei* the police
der Adler the eagle	*das Essen* the food

3.

Jäger the hunter	**fängt** traps
stiehlt robs	**nimmt fest** arrests

4.

schlukt swallows	**der Adler und der Dieb** the eagle & the thief
die Polizei und der Jäger the police & the hunter	**die Frau und das Essen** the woman & the food

5.

die Polizei nimmt fest the police arrest	**der Adler frißt** the eagle eats
der Dieb stiehlt the thief robs	**die Katze fängt** the cat traps

6.

die Schlange schlukt the snake swallows	**die Maus frißt das Essen** the mouse eats the food
der Adler greift an the eagle attacks	**der Jäger tötet** the hunter kills

7.

der Dieb ist in Gefängnis the thief is in prison	**die Frau macht das Essen** the woman prepares the food
die Katze fängt die Maus the cat traps the mouse	**die Schlange schlukt die Katze** the snake swallows the cat

8.

der Adler the eagle	**der Jäger fängt die Maus** the hunter traps the mouse
der Dieb stiehlt den Adler the thief robs the eagle	**die Polizei nimmt den Dieb fest** the police arrest the thief

 Turn the audio off.

Performance Challenge:

Draw a scene from the vocabulary you learned in your Match and Learn exercise. After you draw your picture, describe each part of the scene to a parent, friend, or one of your brothers and sisters. Remember to use as much German as you can to talk about your drawing. For an even greater challenge, use the different words you've learned to create sentences. You can either write the sentences or make picture sentences by drawing your own versions of the pictures from the Match and Learn activity.

The Hunter and the Thief I

(Diglot Weave)

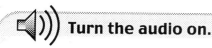 **Turn the audio on.**

Track 6

Narrator: Your Onkel drives through the city. Although the city looks old, it is still a surprise when you come in sight of the Schloss, which looks old-fashioned and out of place surrounded by the city.

Lisa: This is amazing!

Otto: Yes, Lisa. This Schloss has had an interesting history. It was built as a town hall in the sixteenth century, and was expanded to the Ducal Schloss in the eighteen hundreds. It's an interesting mix of styles, much like Luxembourg itself.

Tony: It's enormous! How will we know where to look?

Otto: Well, let's go inside and look around, then we can see if we see anything from the story.

Lisa: Will you tell us the whole story, Onkel Otto, so we know what to look for?

Otto: I think you're ready for a simple version of the story. Listen closely.

Dies ist meine Geschichte:

Track 7

Erste, macht die Frau das Essen.
Here is die Frau preparing das Essen.

Dann kommt die Maus und frißt das Essen.
Here is die Maus eating das Essen.

Dann kommt die Katze und fängt die Maus.
Here is die Katze catching die Maus.

Dann kommt die Schlange und schluckt die Katze.
Here is die Schlange swallowing die Katze.

Dann kommt der Adler und greift die Schlange an.

Here is der Adler attacking die Schlange.

Dann kommt der Jäger und tötet den Adler.

Here is der Jäger killing den Adler.

Dann kommt der Dieb und stiehlt den Adler.

Here is der Dieb stealing den Adler.

Dann kommt die Polizei und nimmt den Dieb fest.

Here is die Polizei arresting den Dieb.

Und der Dieb geht ins Gefängnis.

Und hier ist der Dieb im Gefängnis.

Poor Frau! Poor Maus!

Poor Katze! Poor Schlange!

Poor Adler! Poor Jäger!

Und poor Dieb!

 Turn the audio off.

Performance Challenge:

There are four parts to this Performance Challenge:
1. Read the story silently to yourself.
2. Read the story aloud to yourself.
3. Read the story aloud to a parent, friend or one of your brothers and sisters.
4. Retell the story in your own words, using as much German as you can, to a parent, friend or one of your brothers and sisters.
Don't worry if you can't remember every word. Do the best you can, and review the audio if you need to.
For an even greater challenge, write the next chapter for each diglot weave. If the story hadn't ended, what would happen next?

The Hunter and the Thief I

(Review Questions)

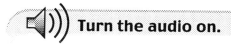 **Turn the audio on.**

Track 8

Narrator: After listening to your Onkel's story, you all split up and begin to explore the Schloss. Although you are very interested in all the old art and artifacts in the Schloss, you begin to be discouraged when you don't find anything right away.

Tony: Do you think we'll ever find Hans, Lisa?

Lisa: I'm not sure. I don't even know what he looks like.

Tony: Let's go and find Onkel Otto. He'll probably know better than we do where to search.

Narrator: You both set off to find your Onkel, but find yourself becoming lost in the twisting hallways and rooms of the Schloss. You are debating whether to turn right or left when you hear a familiar voice down the hall.

Nikolaus: Komm, Hans, Ich werde langsam müde. Gehen wir!

Tony: Did you hear that, Lisa?

Lisa: It sounded like Nikolaus!

Narrator: You both quickly duck into an empty room and peer around the door just as you see Nikolaus and a small brown-haired man you don't recognize, walk past.

Tony: That must be Hans! Quick, let's go find Onkel Otto.

Narrator: You scurry out of the room and down a hallway, where you find your Onkel looking at a painting. You tell him what you saw, and he is concerned.

Otto: I'm worried. If he has Nikolaus with him, we may not be able to speak to him alone.

Lisa: We have to know what room he wanted to meet us in!

Otto: You're right, Lisa. Do you think you understood the story well enough to know what to look for?

Tony: I think we did.

Otto: Okay, to see how much you understood, I'm going to ask you some questions about the story, and see if you can answer in German. Listen.

Note: Review questions are audio only.

 Turn the audio off.

The Hunter and the Thief II

(Diglot Weave)

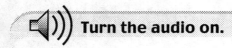 **Turn the audio on.**

Otto: You understood the story well. Let's go outside in the gardens and look around some more.

Narrator: Encouraged, you all walk to the gardens, which are lovely. You search the gardens but find nothing useful, and then sit on a bench in the fading sunlight.

Lisa: It's getting late, Onkel Otto. Do you think we'll find Hans before we have to go?

Otto: I hope so. Do you think you're ready to hear the full version of the story, so that we all know what to look for?

Tony: I think we are.

Otto: Okay. Listen carefully. Remember, you don't have to understand every word to understand the story.

Der Jäger und der Dieb

Bald we're going to see wie you learned die Geschichte.

Was geschah zuerst?

Die Frau Machte das Essen.

Hier, macht die Frau das Essen.

Was geschah dann?

Dann fraß die Maus das Essen.

Hier, frißt die Maus das Essen

Was geschah dann?

Dann kam die Katze und fing die Maus.

Hier fängt die Katze die Maus.

Was geschah dann?

Dann kam die Schlange und schluckte die Katze.

Hier schluckt die Schlange die Katze.

Was geschah dann?

Dann kam der Adler und friff die Schlange an.

Hier greift der Adler die Schlange an.

Was geschah dann?

Dann kam der Jäger und tötete den Adler.

Hier töten der Jäger den Adler.

Was geschah dann?

Dann kam der Dieb und stahl den Adler.

Hier stiehlt der Dieb den Adler.

Was geschah dann?

Dann kam die Polizei und nahm den Dieb fest.

Hier nimmt die Polizei den Dieb fest.

Was geschah dann?

Der Deib ging ins Gefängnis.

Und hier geht der Dieb ins Gefängnis.

 Turn the audio off.

Performance Challenge:

There are four parts to this Performance Challenge:

1. Read the story silently to yourself.
2. Read the story aloud to yourself.
3. Read the story aloud to a parent, friend or one of your brothers and sisters.
4. Retell the story in your own words, using as much German as you can, to a parent, friend or one of your brothers and sisters. Don't worry if you can't remember every word. Do the best you can, and review the audio if you need to.

For an even greater challenge, write the next chapter for each diglot weave. If the story hadn't ended, what would happen next?

The Hunter and the Thief II

(Story Telling)

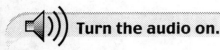 **Turn the audio on.**

Narrator: After searching for some time, you all decide that Hans isn't in the garden. You all head back inside, worried that you might not have time to find him before the Schloss closes. You find yourself searching rooms you have already been in, and wonder if you will ever find the next clue.

Lisa: Let's go over the clue that Hans gave us over the phone again. What was it?

Otto: It was, "Triff mich im Grand Ducal Schloss, wohin der Dieb geht." Do you understand what it means?

Tony: Well, I understand some of the words, like Dieb. I'm sure the answer is in the story somewhere.

Otto: I have an idea. So that we can go over the story again, and I can see how much you understand, I want you to tell the story back to me again, using as much German as you can. Okay?

 Turn the audio off.

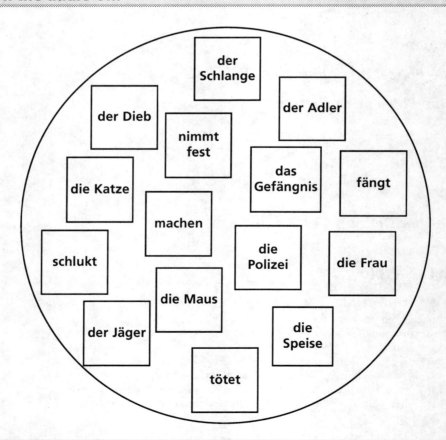

Word Puzzle 3

(The Hunter and the Thief)

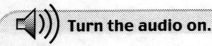 **Turn the audio on.**

Track 12

Otto: Now, we need to know where the Dieb goes, right?

Tony: Right, at the end the Polizei catches him, and he goes to…

Lisa: Gefängnis. Right? Is there a Gefängnis in the Schloss?

Narrator: Your Onkel asks the curator if there is a jail in the Schloss, and he tells you how to find the room where they used to keep prisoners when the Schloss was a town hall. Excited, you all race down to the room, to see if Hans is there. When you arrive, however, the room is empty.

Otto: We must have missed him. He must have already gone.

Lisa: But, Tony, Onkel Otto, look!

Narrator: On the ground you see a piece of paper, as if someone has dropped it. When you pick it up, you see that it is a puzzle.

Otto: What do you suppose this is?

Tony: It must be a clue! Hans must have left it for us. Look, it used words from "Der Jäger und der Dieb." Let's see if we can solve it.

 Turn the audio off.

Fill in the blanks in the puzzle below by following the numbered clues. The letters that fall in the circled blanks will make additional words that will help you on your adventure.

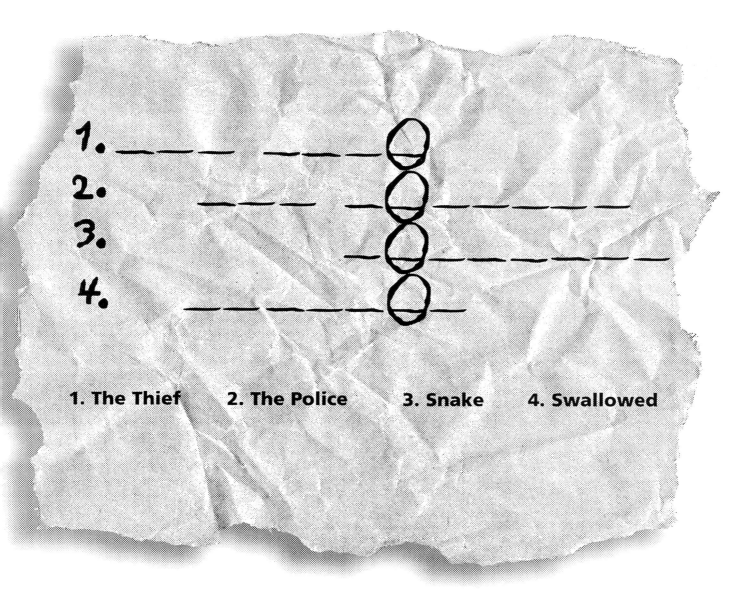

1. The Thief   2. The Police   3. Snake   4. Swallowed

A Boy and His Goat

(Scatter Chart)

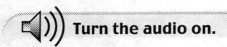 **Turn the audio on.**

Tony: The puzzle says "Bock." What's a Bock, Onkel Otto?

Otto: Not a thing, Tony, a place. The Bock is a large, rocky outcropping right here in Luxembourg City. Sigefroid, Count of Ardennes, built a fortress there many years ago. The fortress is long gone, but ruins still remain, and they're a marvelous place to hide things.

Lisa: I'll bet that's where Hans wants to meet us! Maybe he can get away from Nikolaus long enough to tell us where Nikolaus is keeping the music.

Tony: Or maybe it's a trap. Any place that good for hiding things has to be pretty good for hiding people, too.

Otto: Well, that is a chance I think we will have to take if we want to get the music back. Will you kommen mit mir?

Lisa: Of course, Onkel Otto!

Tony: Ja!

Lisa: What sort of clue do you think Hans will give us this time?

Otto: Let me think… Ah, yes. When we were exploring the ruins, our guide told us a charming story about a boy and his goat. I believe Hans will probably use that story in his clue.

Tony: Will you teach it to us?

Otto: It's a fairly difficult story. I think I should teach you a few of the words that are in it first.

Look at the pictures on your workbook page and point to what you hear.

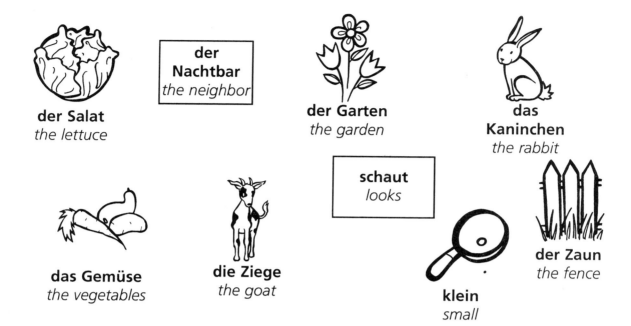

der Salat
the lettuce

der Nachtbar
the neighbor

der Garten
the garden

das Kaninchen
the rabbit

das Gemüse
the vegetables

die Ziege
the goat

schaut
looks

klein
small

der Zaun
the fence

 Turn the audio off.

Performance Challenge:

Choose five of the new words and pictures that you learned in the Scatter Chart. Show the pictures to a parent, friend, or one of your brothers and sisters and explain to them how you think the picture represents the words you have learned. For an even greater challenge, create your own story using the pictures. Bring out the artist in yourself by drawing your own versions of the pictographs and making a book with the story you create.

A Boy and His Goat I
(Diglot Weave)

 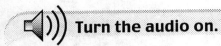 **Turn the audio on.**

Lisa: Okay, we know those words. Will you tell us the story now?

Otto: All right. I will tell you the simpler version of the story first.

Tony: Can we start going to the Bock while you're telling us? I really don't want to miss Hans again.

Otto: That's a fine idea, Tony. Let's go back to the car, and I'll tell it to you while I drive.

Der Junge und Seine Ziege
Es war einman ein Junge namens Paul. Er had a goat die den Garten des Nachbarn begehrte.

Each Tag Paul went with seiner Ziege zu der pasture in der Nähe des Hauses des Nachbarn. There die Ziege ate das sweet grass.

Und each day, as they an dem Haus des Nachbarn vorbei gingen, die Ziege looked longingly auf den Garten.

Several Male she tried to break down den fence so she could in dem Garten gehen und das Gemüse essen. Der lettuce seemed besonders lecker.

Eines Tages as Paul led seine Ziege zur Wiese, they gingen an dem Garten vorbei und die Ziege stoß den Zaun mit ihren horns und broke it.

Immediately lief die Ziege und begann den leckeren Salat zu essen.

Paul tugged am Seil with all seiner Kraft. He shouted und whistled, aber die Ziege didn't pay attention...sie ignoreirte ihn. He wouldn't even lift ihren Kopf. She just kept on die Salatblätter zu fressen.

Mit all seiner Kraft Paul tried to remove die Ziege vom Garten, aber he couldn't.

Endlich setze er sich hin und began zu weinem.

By chance, in dem Augenblick, kam ein kleines Kaninchen vorbei.

"Tag, Junge. Warum weinst du?"

"Ich weine, weil meine Ziege brach den Zaun des Nachbarn zerbrach. Nun frißt sie sein Gemüse, und ich kann nicht get her out. I can't even get him to raise ihren Kopf."

"Well das shouldn't be so schwer; I'll do it."

Das Kaninchen sprang vor die Ziege und rief, "Hallo, Ziege, look zu mir!"

Das Kaininchen flopped seine Ohren und sprang und hüpfte und schrie, "Hallo, du! Hallo, du! Schau zu mir!"

But die Ziege didn't pay any attention…sie ignoreirte es einfach. She wouldn't even ihren Kopf heban, instead he kept on den Salat zu fressen.

Finally das Kaninchen gave up und setze sich neben Paul, und he began zu weinen.

In dem Augenblick, kam eine Füchsin vorbei proudly, lifting ihren Schwanz high so that everyone could admire it.

"Hallo, Kaninchen, warum weinst du?"

"Ich weine, weil die Ziege didn't pay attention to me, und der Junge weint, weil seine Ziege den Zaun des Nachbarn zerbrach und jetzt sein gemüse frißt, und er can't get die Ziege to come out."

"Naja," sagte Frau Fuchsin, "Ich sehe darin kein Problem. So, if you don't mind, ich werde es machen."

Then Frau Fuchsin lief zu der Ziege und began to walk vor ihr. All the time saying, "Hallo, Ziege, schau zu mir!"

Aber die Ziege war es egal. He wouldn't even ihren Kopf heben. He just kept den Salat zu fressen.

Finally Frau Fuchsin gave up und setzte sich hin und began zu weinen beside dem Kaninchen.

In dem Augenblick, kam ein großer und prideful Wolf vorbei.

"Frau Fuchsin, warum weinst du? Und warum weinen die anderen?"

"Ich weine aus dem selben Grund wie das Kaninchen, und das Kaninchen weint aus dem selben Grund wie der Junge."

"Und warum weint der Junge?

"Der Junge weint, weil seine Ziege den Zaun des Nachbarn zerbrach und den Salat frißt. Und nun kann er die Ziege nicht remove."

"Naja, ich sehe da kein Problem. Ich kann es machen."

Der große Wolf went zum Garten und knurrte die Ziege an, "Grrrrr," and made faces zu der Ziege und even blies und püstetet.

Aber die Ziege war es egal, und sie hob nicht einmal den Kopf. She just fraß weiter den Salat.

Also setzte der Wolf setzte sich hin und begann zu weinen.

In dem Augenblick, flog eine Horniße vorbei.

"Wolf, warum weinst du?"

"Na, ich weine aus dem selben Grund wie der Fuchs, und der Fuchs weint aus dem selben Grund wie das Kaninchen, und das Kaninchen weint aus dem selben Grund wie der Junge."

"Und warum weint der Junge?"

"Der Junge weint, weil seine Ziege den Zaun des Nachbarn zerbrach und den Salat frißt. Now he can't get die Ziege to come out, oder nicht einmal dem Kopf zu heben."

"Naja, ich sehe darin kein Problem. Ich kann es," sagte die Hornisse. "Ich can remove die Ziege vom Garten."

In dem Augenblick they all stopped weinen. A hornet so klein was going to die Ziege vom Garten treiben? Wie could it be?

Alle watched while die Hornisse flew over to die Ziege. Sie flew an den Ohren der Ziege vorbei und finally he landed auf seiner Nase.

Then begann die Hornisse to dance auf der Nase der Ziege, und das tickled die Nase der Ziege, und die Ziege began to laugh, "haa, haa. . .ha, ha," until he realized what was tickling his nose.

"EINE HORNISSE!" Die Ziege sprang in die Luft, und die Hornisse stung her auf die Nase, und die Ziege rannte aus den Garten.

Die Hornisse flew away, der Wolf slunk down die Straße, der Fuchs lief zu der Wiese, und das Kaninchen sprang, und das ist das Ende.

 Turn the audio off.

Performance Challenge:

There are four parts to this Performance Challenge:
1. Read the story silently to yourself.
2. Read the story aloud to yourself.
3. Read the story aloud to a parent, friend or one of your brothers and sisters.
4. Retell the story in your own words, using as much German as you can, to a parent, friend or one of your brothers and sisters.
Don't worry if you can't remember every word. Do the best you can, and review the audio if you need to.
For an even greater challenge, write the next chapter for each diglot weave. If the story hadn't ended, what would happen next?

A Boy and His Goat
(*Review Questions*)

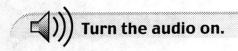 **Turn the audio on.**

Track 17

Otto: Well, here we are: the Bock.

Tony: What's that over there, Onkel Otto?

Otto: That's an entrance to the casemates, Tony.

Lisa: Casemates?

Otto: Yes, that's right. The casemates were built in the seventeenth century. They're a series of tunnels and chambers that go underground, sometimes as much as forty meters deep!

Tony: Wow! What did people do with them?

Otto: Well, at first they were used for defense. They made the fortress very hard to conquer. During World War I and World War II, they were used for bomb shelters. Historians estimate these casemates sheltered as many as 35,000 people.

Lisa: They must be really big! Do you really think we'll be able to find Hans inside them?

Tony: We have to. It's the only way we'll get that music back where it belongs.

Otto: Tony's right, it's our best chance. Come on, I'll ask you some review questions while we walk.

Note: Review questions are audio only.

 Turn the audio off.

A Boy and His Goat II

(Diglot Weave)

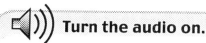 **Turn the audio on.**

Track 18

Lisa: It's cold in here.

Tony: Of course it is, it's underground. I don't see any sign of Hans yet, though.

Otto: Well, we haven't gone very far... Ssh! What's that?

Lisa: It sounds like someone coming this way!

Narrator: You all duck into a damp underground chamber. There's barely room for all of you. You wait in the darkness as the voice draws closer.

Tony: That's Nikolaus! I recognize his voice!

Narrator: Sure enough, mere seconds later, Nikolaus passes, carrying a lantern and muttering in German about where Hans disappeared to this time. He passes without seeing you and stalks toward the entrance.

Tony: Whew! That was close.

Lisa: Well, at least we know we're on the right trail.

Otto: Nikolaus is gone now. Let's keep going. I can tell you the second version of the story while we walk.

Ein Junge und Seine Ziege

Track 19

Es war einmal ein Junge namens Paul. Er hatte eine Ziege die dem Garten des Nachbarn begehrte.

Jeden Tag, Paul took seiner Zeige zu der Wiese in der nähe des Hauses des Nachbarn.

Da, fraß die Ziege das Gras.

Und jeden Tag, als sie an dem Haus des Nachbarn vorbei gingen, schaute die Ziege begehrig auf den Garten.

Ein Paar Male, versuchte die Ziege durch den Zaun zu brechen, um das Gemüse zu freßen. Das Salat schien besonders lecker.

Eines Tages, als Paul zur Wiese mit der Ziege ging, gingen sie an dem Garten vorbei, und die Ziege zerbrach den Zaun mit ihren Hörnern.

So fort, lief die Ziege und begann den leckeren Salat zu essen.

Paul zog am Seil mit alle seiner Kraft. Er schrie und rief, aber die Ziege war es egal, die hob nicht einmal den Kopf, und sie fraß weiter hin die Salatblätter.

Paul versuchte mit all seiner Kraft die Ziege vom Garten zu entfernen , aber er konnte es nicht.

Schlieslich, setze er sich hin und begann zu weinen.

In dem Augenblick, kam ein kleines Kaninchen vorbei.

"Hallo, Junge ! Warum weinst du?"

"Ich weine, weil meine Ziege den Zaun des Nachbarn zerbrach und jetzt sein Gemüse frißt, und ich kann sie nicht zurück holen, sie wird nicht einmal den Kopf heben. "

"Naja, das soll nicht so schwer sein. Ich werde es machen."

Das Kaninchen sprang vor die Ziege und rief, "Hallo, Ziege, schau zu mir!"

Das Kaninchen flatterte seine Ohren und sprang und hüpfte und schrie, "Hallo, du ! Hallo, du! Schau zu mir!"

Aber die Ziege sie war es egal, sie hat nicht einmal den Kopf gehoben. Sie fraßt weiterhin den Salat.

Endlich, gab das Kaninchen auf und setzte sich neben Paul und begann zu weinen.

In dem Augenblick, kam eine stolze Füchsin vorbei, raising ihren Schwanz daß jeder sie bewundern konnte.

"Hallo, Kaninchen, warum weinst du?"

"Ich weine, weil die Ziege mich ignorierte, und der Junge weint, weil seine Ziege den Zaun des Nachbarn zerbrach und den Salat frißt, und er kann sie zurück holen."

"Naja," sagte Frau Fuchsin, "Ich sehe darin kein Problem. Wenn es dich nicht stört, werde ich es machen."

Dann lief Frau Fuchsin zu der Ziege und begann vor ihr zu gehen , sagend, "Hallo, Ziege, schau zu mir."

Aber die Ziege war es egal, und sie hob nicht einmal den Kopf. Sie fraß weiterhin den Salat.

Endlich, gab Frau Fuchsin auf, setzte sich neben dem Kaninchen und begann zu weinen.

In dem Augenblick, kam ein großer und stolzer Wolf vorbei.

"Frau Fuchsin, warum weinst du? Und warum weinen die anderen?"

"Ich weine aus dem selben Grund wie das Kaninchen, und das Kaninchen weint aus dem selben Grund wie der Junge."

"Und warum weint der Junge?"

"Der Junge weint, weil seine Ziege den Zaun des Nachbarn zerbrach und den Salat frißt . Nun kann er die Ziege nicht zurück holen, und sie will nicht einmal den Kopf heben. "

"Naja, ich sehe darin kein Problem Ich kann es machen."

Der große Wolf ging zum Garten und knurrte die Ziege an, Grrrr, und blies und püstetet.

Aber die Ziege war es egal, sie hob nicht einmal den Kopf. Sie fraß weiterhin den Salat .

Und der Wolf setzte sich hin und begann zu weinen.

In dem Augenblick, flog eine Hornisse vorbei.

"Wolf, warum weinst du?"

"Na, ich weine aus dem selben Grund wie der Fuchs, und der Fuchs weint aus dem selben Grund wie das Kaninchen, und das Kaninchen weint aus dem selben Grund wie der Junge."

"Und warum weint der Junge?"

"Der Junge weint, weil seine Ziege den Zaun des Nachbarn zerbrach und den Salat frißt. Und er kann die Ziege nicht zurück holen, sie will nicht einmal den Kopf heben."

"Naja, ich sehe dorin kein Problem. Ich kann es," sagte die Hornisse. "Ich werde die Ziege vom Garten treiben."

In dem Augenblick, alle die Tiere stoppte weinen. "Eine Hornisse so klein wird die Ziege vom Garten treiben? Wie ist das möglich?"

Alle die Tiere schauten wie die Hornisse zu der Ziege flog. Sie flog an den Ohren der Ziege vorbei und landete auf ihrer Nase.

Dann begann die Hornisse auf der Nase der Ziege zu tanzen. Das kitzelte die Ziege, und er lachte, "Ha, ha, ha, ha !" bis sie sah, was auf ihre Nase tanzte .

"EINE HORNISSE!" Die Ziege sprang in die Luft. Die Hornisse stach die Ziege auf die Nase, und die Ziege rannte aus den Garten.

Der Wolf schleichke die Straße rünter, der Fuchs lief zu der Wiese, das Kaninchen sprang darin, und das ist das Ende.

 Turn the audio off.

Performance Challenge:

There are four parts to this Performance Challenge:

1. Read the story silently to yourself.
2. Read the story aloud to yourself.
3. Read the story aloud to a parent, friend or one of your brothers and sisters.
4. Retell the story in your own words, using as much German as you can, to a parent, friend or one of your brothers and sisters. Don't worry if you can't remember every word. Do the best you can, and review the audio if you need to.

For an even greater challenge, write the next chapter for each diglot weave. If the story hadn't ended, what would happen next?

Word Puzzle 4

(A Boy and His Goat)

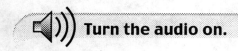 **Turn the audio on.**

Narrator: The tunnel that you have been following comes to an abrupt dead end.

Lisa: Great! Now what do we do?

Tony: Wait, I think I see something. Here, in the rubble by the wall. It's another piece of paper. It looks like it got a little wet just sitting there, but I can still read it.

Lisa: It's another puzzle from Hans. It looks like it uses words we learned from "Der Junge und Seine Ziege."

Tony: Let's give it a try!

 Turn the audio off.

Fill in the blanks in the puzzle below by following the numbered clues. The letters that fall in the circled blanks will make additional words that will help you on your adventure.

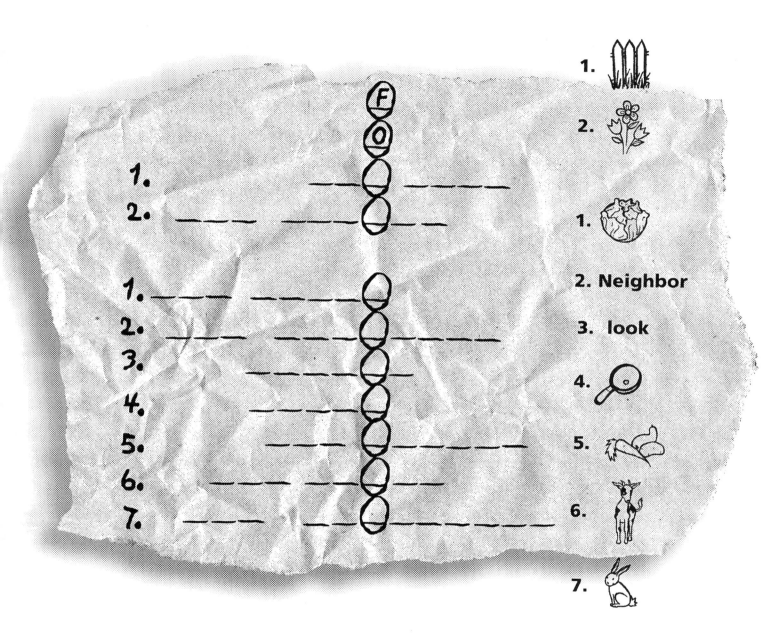

1.

2. Neighbor

3. look

1.

2.

3.

4.

5.

6.

7.

A Sandwich in the Universe

(Horseshoe Story)

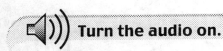 **Turn the audio on.**

Lisa: The puzzle says, "Fort Thungen." What is that?

Otto: Fort Thungen is an old fort outside of the city, here. That must be where Hans wants to meet us next.

Tony: Can we go now?

Otto: It's too late tonight. Let's go back to the hotel.

Narrator: Once back in the hotel, you are too excited to sleep.

Lisa: Have you been to Fort Thungen before, Onkel Otto?

Otto: I have. I went there with Hans the last time we were here together, because we were researching a folklore story.

Tony: What was the story?

Otto: It was called, "Das Sandwich im Zentrum des Universums."

Lisa: Will you teach it to us? I bet that's what Hans will use in his next clue.

Otto: You may be right, Lisa. Listen, and I will tell it to you.

The Sandwich in the Universe

Das ist ein Sandwich.

Das ist das Universum.

Im Universum gibt es eine Galaxie.

In der Galaxie gibt es ein Stern.

Neben dem Stern gibt es eine Erde.

Auf der Erde gibt es einen Kontinent.

Auf dem Kontinent gibt es ein Land.

Im Land gibt es eine Stadt.

In der Stadt gibt es ein Park.

Im Park gibt es ein Junge.

In den Händen des Junge gibt es ein Sandwich.

Ein sandwich in den Händen des Junge,

Der Junge im Park,

Der Park in der Stadt,

Die Stadt im Land,

Das Land auf dem Kontinent,

Der Kontinent auf der Erde,

Die Erde neben dem Stern,

Der Stern in der Galaxie,

Die Galaxie im Universum.

Und hier ist der Sandwich in den Händen des Junge.

 Turn the audio off.

Performance Challenge:

Create hand actions to represent the actions in the horseshoe story. (For example: Make up different actions to represent the animals you heard about in the story.) After you have created the actions, perform your mini-play for a parent, friend, or one of your bothers and sisters. Remember to narrate your actions in German and then translate your words if your audience does not understand German. For an even greater challenge, try writing your own horseshoe story. Choose several things or people that are related to each other in some way. Think of a chain of events that connects the characters in the story. To finish the story, figure out how the events could be reversed in order to back through the pictures and the plot.

A Sandwich in the Universe

(Scatter Chart)

Track 23

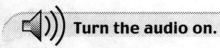 **Turn the audio on.**

Narrator: The next morning you leave for the fort before it is even light out. You reach it just as the sun is coming up and are amazed by how grand and imposing the fort looks in the morning light.

Tony: Do you think we'll be able to find Nikolaus and Hans, Onkel Otto?

Otto: I hope so. I've been thinking about why Nikolaus would come to Luxembourg with the manuscripts, and I think the manuscripts may be in more danger than we realized.

Lisa: What do you mean?

Otto: I think that Nikolaus wants to sell the manuscripts, and that he has found a buyer here in Luxembourg. If he sells the manuscripts, we will probably never find them again.

Tony: That's terrible! We have to find them soon, then!

Otto: I agree. Luckily, we have Hans helping us, and we know all the folklore that he is using. Do you children feel like you understood the story that I told you yesterday?

Lisa: I understood some of it, but there were a lot of words that I didn't recognize.

Tony: Me neither.

Otto: Okay, then, let's go over the words as we go into the fort, so that you can understand the whole story. Okay?

Track 24

Look at the pictures on your workbook page and point to what you hear.

die Galaxie
the galaxy

die Erde
the earth

das Sandwich
the sandwich

der Park
the park

die Stadt
the city

der Junge
the boy

der Kontinent
the continent

das Land
the country

die Hand
the hand

der Stern
the star

 Turn the audio off.

Performance Challenge:

Choose five of the new words and pictures that you learned in the Scatter Chart. Show the pictures to a parent, friend, or one of your brothers and sisters and explain to them how you think the picture represents the words you have learned. For an even greater challenge, create your own story using the pictures. Bring out the artist in yourself by drawing your own versions of the pictographs and making a book with the story you create.

A Sandwich in the Universe

(Story Retelling)

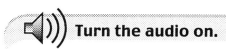 **Turn the audio on.**

Track 25

Narrator: You enter the fort, and a tour guide shows you around. She tells you it was constructed by a man named Baron Van Thungen, which you think sounds like something out of a fairy tale. She also shows you the defense parts of the fort, including a line of cannons up on the roof. You stop to play on the cannons for awhile, and your Onkel watches you.

Tony: This is fun!

Otto: That's all very good, Tony, but I think we need to focus on finding Hans. Do you think you understand the story I told you yet?

Lisa: I think we did.

Otto: Okay, then, I want you to tell the story back to me, using as much German as you can. Remember the words you learned!

 Turn the audio off.

Now retell the story using as much German as you can.

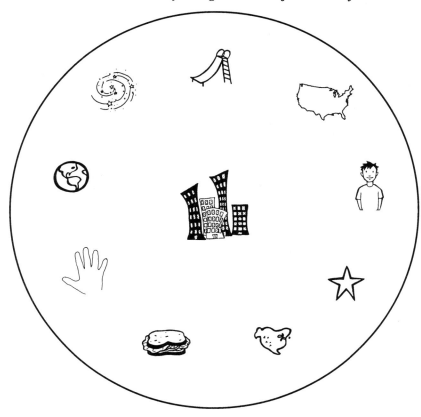

Final Word Puzzle

(A Sandwich in the Universe)

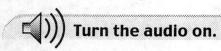 **Turn the audio on.**

Narrator: You all follow the tour guide down to the basement of the fort, where she shows you a long tunnel that was built to go beneath the slimy green moat. You are a little frightened by the dark hole and the thought of all that water over your head. You fall behind the rest of the group as you explore a small passage off to the side. Just then, however, you see Nikolaus and Hans again, walking the other direction, out of the tunnel.

Lisa: Look, Tony! We should go and tell Onkel Otto!

Tony: Shhh! They'll hear you.

Narrator: You press against the wall and try not to be seen as Nikolaus and Hans pass. You see the manuscripts you are searching for tucked under Nikolaus' arm! Nikolaus does not look at you, but Hans sees you, and drops another piece of paper on the floor.

Nikolaus: Beeile dich, Hans, wir müssen den Mann finden, der die Manuskripten kauft.

Narrator: After they pass, you grab the piece of paper that Hans dropped and you run ahead and find your Onkel, telling him what you saw.

Otto: Oh, no. If Nikolaus has the manuscripts with him, it must mean that he is ready to give them to the person who is buying them. He might be here, in this very fort!

Tony: What about this piece of paper that Hans dropped? It might be a clue.

Otto: You're right, Tony, let's take a look.

 Turn the audio off.

Fill in the blanks in the puzzle below by following the numbered clues. The letters that fall in the circled blanks will make additional words that will help you on your adventure.

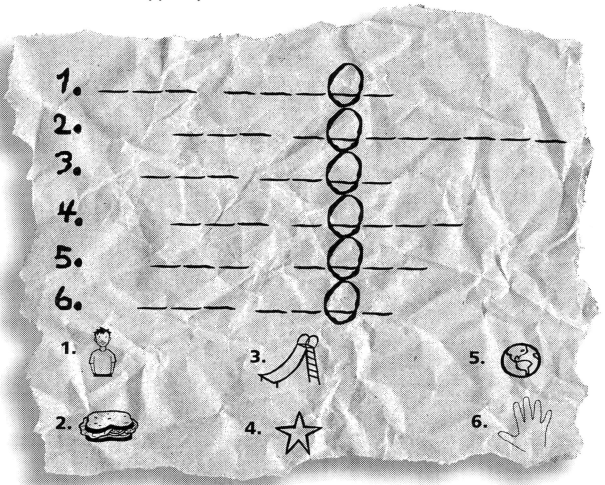

105

Success!

(Manuscripts)

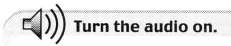 **Turn the audio on.**

Track 27

Lisa: The puzzle says, "Garten." They must be in the garden!

Narrator: You all run up the stairs and out into the garden as quickly as you can. Once there, you begin searching around for Nikolaus and Hans.

Tony: There! There is Nikolaus, right there!

Lisa: Tony, wait! Look, he doesn't have the manuscripts with him any more! He must have already sold them!

Narrator: You all stand still, unsure about what to do next, but just then a tall blond man walks past you, with the manuscripts tucked under his arm.

Otto: Verzeihung! Verzeihung, mein Herr!

Narrator: The man stops and he and your Onkel talk for a moment. The blond man becomes more and more concerned as the conversation goes on. Finally, your Onkel turns to you.

Otto: Tony, Lisa, this is Kristoff. He is a German man who collects ancient manuscripts. He just bought these from Nikolaus, but he did not know that they were stolen. He says he is willing to return them to the museum, and that he knows where Nikolaus is staying so that we can inform the police.

Tony: Yes! The manuscripts are saved!

Lisa: We did it!

 Turn the audio off.

Safe Return

(Mission Accomplished)

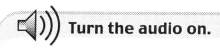 **Turn the audio on.**

Narrator: You are back in Berlin, where your adventure began, and where your Onkel, your cousin Margarethe, and your parents are all throwing you a party for finding the lost manuscripts.

Otto: I must say, children, I couldn't have retrieved those manuscripts without you. Now, Nikolaus is in prison, and the manuscripts are back in the museum, where they belong.

Margarethe: Gute Arbeit, Kinder.

Narrator: Your parents are glad that you enjoyed yourselves, but they are eager to hear how much German you learned while you were in Luxembourg. Your Onkel Otto designs a test to show them all the German you've learned, and if you pass, they've agreed to let you stay with your Onkel and cousin all summer. Excited by the thought of how much you could do and see in Germany over a whole summer, you decide to take the test.

 Turn the audio off.

Test 2

🔊))) **Turn the audio on.**

A. Frame Identifications

For each question, you will see a box with pictures. You will hear a statement about one of the pictures. There will be a pause of 10 seconds to identify the picture, and then the statement will be repeated.

1.

2.

3.

the eagle	the woman
the thief	the food

4.

the police	the eagle
the thief	the hunter

5.

Comprehension Multiple-Choice

Complete the following conversations by choosing the correct answer from the options listed.

1. "Sophie! Ich freue mich, dich zu sehen. Lass mich dir meine Enkelkinder vorstellen"

    A. Es freut mich, sie kennen zu lernen.

    B. Gut gemacht!

    C. Gehen wir hier.

    D. Bitte schön.

2. Who owned den Garten mit Salat?

    A. der Junge

    B. die Ziege

    C. der Nachbar

    D. der Fuchs

3. Was ist zuerst geschehen?

    A. Die Katze fängt die Maus.

    B. Die Frau macht die Speise.

    C. Der Jäger fiel auf die Schlange.

    D. Die Polizei hat den Dieb fest genommen.

4. Wo ist die Galaxie?

    A. in dem Park

    B. in der Stadt

    C. in dem Land

    D. in dem Universum

5. Warum weinst du?

    A. Gut gemacht! Ich esse die Speise.

    B. Es freut mich dich kennen zu lernen. Weisst du, wo ich eine von denen finden kann?

    C. Die Ziege hat den Zaun des Nachbarn kaputt gemacht, und den Salat gefressen.

    D. Na ja, ich sehe kein Problem hier.

Now go on to complete the reading/writing portion of this test.

 Turn the audio off.

Matching

Choose the statements that match and draw a line to connect the two.

1. lettuce	a. der Garten
2. fence	b. der Kontinent
3. garden	c. der Salat
4. continent	d. der Adler
5. eagle	e. der Zaun

True or False

Write T or F for each statement.

_____ 1. Der Dieb arrests die Polizei und puts him in Gefängnis.

_____ 2. Die Ziege in der Geschichte is afraid of die Hornisse.

_____ 3. Der Nachbar has den Salat in seinem Garten.

_____4. Der Jäger eats den Adler.

___ 5. When none of the andere Tiere knew what to do, die Hornisse saved the day.

Answer Key

1.

2.

3.

the eagle	the woman
the thief	the food

4.

the police	the eagle
the thief	the hunter

5.

Comprehension Multiple-Choice

1. A
2. C
3. B.
4. D.
5. C

Matching

1. B
2. E

3. A
4. B
5. D

True or False

1. F
2. T
3. T
4. F
5. T

Recipes

BLACK FOREST CAKE

1 box chocolate cake mix

1 1/4 cups fruit juice (apple, cranberry, or cherry is good)

3 eggs

1/4 cup vegetable oil

1 can cherry pie filling

1/4 cup water

2 teaspoons cornstarch

1/2 teaspoon almond extract (optional)

1 carton (16 oz.) whipped topping (can substitute 1/2 pint whipped cream, whipped and sweetened with 1 tablespoon sugar and 1/2 teaspoon vanilla)

2 tablespoons chocolate syrup

1 jar (7 oz.) marshmallow creme

Combine cake mix, fruit juice, eggs, and vegetable oil and beat together for two minutes. Bake in greased and floured 9 x 13 x 2 inch pan for 30 minutes, or until cake tests done. Let cool, then slice in half horizontally to form two layers.

In a saucepan, while the cake is cooling, combine cherry pie filling, water, and cornstarch. Simmer until thick, then remove from heat. Stir in almond extract, if desired. Let cool completely.

Combine whipped topping, chocolate syrup, and marshmallow cream in a large bowl. Beat until thoroughly combined.

To assemble: Spread the bottom layer of the cake with 1/3 of the whipped topping mix. Spread 1/2 of the cherry mix on top of the whipped topping mix. Top with the remaining layer of cake. Spread the remaining whipped topping mix over the top and sides of the cake. Scoop the remaining cherry mix onto the top of the cake. If desired, garnish top and sides with grated chocolate. Refrigerate leftovers.

LA BOUNESCHLUPP

3 cups long French beans

2 quarts water

4 bouillon cubes

1 carrot, sliced

1 onion, chopped

1 leek, sliced

2 stalks celery, sliced

4 large potatoes, cubed

1 cup lard (optional)

1 cup milk

1/2 cup cream

salt and pepper to taste

Combine the beans, water, and bouillon cubes. Simmer until beans are tender. Add vegetables, and simmer until potatoes are tender. Add lard a little at a time. Add milk and cream, and stir until lard is dissolved. Add salt and pepper to taste. Serve warm with potato crepes.